Daniel Lane started covering Danny Green's boxing career as editor of the 2000 Australian Olympic team's official newsletter, *Aspire*. He is a multi-award-winning journalist, currently employed as the deputy sports editor of *The Sun-Herald*. Lane has worked as a journalist for magazines, radio and television since 1985. *Closed Fists, Open Heart* is his tenth book. He lives in Sydney with Camille.

CLOSED FISTS, OPEN HEART

THE DANNY GREEN STORY

DANNY GREEN with DANIEL LANE

ABC
Books

The ABC 'Wave' device is a trademark of the Australian Broadcasting Corporation and is used under licence by HarperCollins*Publishers* Australia.

This edition first published in 2008 by ABC Books for the Australian Broadcasting Corporation.
Reprinted by HarperCollins*Publishers* Australia Pty Limited
ABN 36 009 913 517
harpercollins.com.au

Copyright © Daniel Lane and Danny Green 2008

The right of Daniel Lane and Danny Green to be identified as the authors of this work has been asserted by them in accordance with the *Copyright Amendment (Moral Rights) Act 2000*.

This work is copyright. Apart from any use as permitted under the *Copyright Act 1968*, no part may be reproduced, copied, scanned, stored in a retrieval system, recorded, or transmitted, in any form or by any means, without the prior written permission of the publisher.

HarperCollins*Publishers*
Level 13, 201 Elizabeth Street, Sydney, NSW 2000, Australia
31 View Road, Glenfield, Auckland 0627, New Zealand
1–A Hamilton House, Connaught Place, New Delhi – 110 001, India
77–85 Fulham Palace Road, London W6 8JB, United Kingdom
2 Bloor Street East, 20th floor, Toronto, Ontario M4W 1A8, Canada
10 East 53rd Street, New York NY 10022, USA

ISBN 978 0 7333 2247 1

Cover design by Luke Causby/Blue Cork
Internal Design by Darian Causby/Highway 51
Typeset in 11.5 by 18pt Sabon by Kirby Jones

I will tell my newborn son Archie exactly what I have told my beautiful daughter Chloe and that is; it's how hard you try that counts. It is the philosophy I have adopted while going about my profession as a fighter, and I'll continue to live it long after I hang my gloves up. I take great pride in knowing I have never shirked an issue; I have never taken a backwards step and I have never given up. I have to look at myself in the mirror knowing I gave all I had to give. And, I have …

This book is dedicated to my lovely family and friends. You are my life.

Danny Green, March 2008

CONTENTS

1. Champion of the world — 1
2. The humanity of boxing — 7
3. Growing pains — 13
4. Dust up and dust off — 19
5. Pat — 26
6. Mighty Marist — 31
7. First blood — 36
8. Riding the thunder — 39
9. Nina — 44
10. Chloe — 50
11. Amateur hour — 57
12. Meeting Ali — 65
13. The boy from Brazil — 69
14. The beast from the east — 73
15. Beaten by a nose — 79
16. The world champion flatmate — 86
17. The Team — 90
18. Showdown in Bankstown — 97
19. Daniel in the lion's den — 100
20. Suffering for the art — 104
21. Hunger — 109
22. Opportunity rings — 114
23. The Challenger — 119
24. Mugged in Germany — 125
25. The bitterest blow — 131

26.	Tom McGuire	135
27.	The brawl in Montreal	138
28.	The twilight zone	144
29.	Is 'dat' a gun in your pocket?	151
30.	T for Terrific	157
31.	Danny Decked	160
32.	Campaign of the lost	163
33.	Wilcannia	168
34.	Jeff Fenech	174
35.	Salas	184
36.	The Electric Eels	189
37.	Dents in the steel spine	196
38.	Life's a million to one shot	200
39.	Mundine madness	204
40.	Fright night	212
41.	A very private pain	222
42.	Bush bashed	225
43.	Sophie Delezio	229
44.	The need for speed	233
45.	Damo	236
46.	The quick green fox	244
47.	One door closes …	251
48.	Heavyweight support	260
49.	The Green Machine	270
50.	Fight Record	275

CHAPTER 1

CHAMPION OF THE WORLD

Three minutes.

What's three minutes out of an hour? Of a day? Of someone's life? On this Perth night, 16 December 2007, three minutes is an eternity for my family and me because it is make or break for us. I circle my opponent Stipe Drews knowing the next three minutes is what stands between me and winning the World Boxing Association's world title and fulfilling my long-held dream to be the official champion of the world.

My trainer Ismael Salas and chief corner man Angelo Hyder have assured me I've won each of the previous 11 rounds against the Croatian, who is 15 centimetres taller than me, and while my heart thumps with excitement one thought runs through my mind as I watch the champion move in to try and save the crown from slipping off his head: 'Don't blow it. Don't blow it now.'

I have been in Drews's boots before, needing to find a knockout punch to win a world title. It's a desperate feeling.

I know he has to give everything he can muster. If he doesn't he'll have to live with the consequences of a few bad minutes for the rest of his life. I know that was what crossed my mind in the final round of my fight against Germany's World Boxing Council super-middleweight champion Markus Beyer two years earlier. I was behind on points and rattled the champion with a heavy blow. I saw fear in Beyer's eyes when he realised he was in danger of losing everything he'd bled for.

Yes, I want to knock Drews out, to make the victory complete, but the safety first thoughts that buzz through my head force me to go against my nature. I think of the many sacrifices, the numerous ups and downs my family has been through as I've chased the world title. I don't need to be gung ho this time. No need to be the hero. *'Don't blow it, mate. Don't blow it.'*

I worry about walking into a big punch so I keep away from Drews as he advances towards me like a big daddy long legs spider chasing a mosquito. I want to finish him off but a voice inside my head tells me not to be reckless this time. I know I've fought a strong and tactically smart fight. I'm happy to know I took this man's heart in the opening two rounds when I rocked him with some heavy blows that hurt him and instilled fear into him. Yet, I am surprised to think that because in front of me stands the reigning world light-heavyweight champion who'd only lost one of his 33 professional contests and was a quarter finalist in the 1996 Atlanta Olympics. There was no respite from my early assault. I fulfilled my pre-fight pledge to go the 'hammer' on him from the start. And I mean *hammer* because Salas had wrapped my hands so tightly and so compact they were rightly described as 'nasty' by a WBA official who oversaw the process of my fists being bandaged. Salas gave me an unfair advantage that night, though it was a perfectly legal one. Regardless, Drews would have been well within his rights to demand for my gloves to be inspected after the bout for two hidden horseshoes such was the power I generated throughout the 12 rounds.

I threw my well-rehearsed combination: two left jabs to make him raise his hands to cover his face and then a right-left-right combination that sunk deep into his body. I walked through him, never taking a backwards step, and what I saw was a man who didn't expect to be stung by such power. After the fight Drews said he couldn't believe he was out-jabbed throughout the bout because not only was it his speciality, but he also enjoyed an incredible height advantage over me. The jab, however, was always my bread and butter — and I force-fed him plenty that summer night.

In the second round I wobbled Drews so hard his eyes rattled. He was getting hurt every time I punched him so he resorted to wrestling for the rest of the fight — locking my arms up and making it difficult for me to punch him. It was horrible as he put me in headlocks and choked me. Yet every time he held me I threw him off and followed the move with wild blows that hurt him. I had prepared myself for this at training. I drummed it into myself to the point where it became instinctive. I knew my aggression and my animosity would rattle him, especially when it was combined with my punching power. Allied with that was the 16 years I'd prepared for this fateful night. My build up for the WBA campaign in the previous eight weeks was brilliant. I'd trained twice a day, six days a week and my whole existence was consumed by the simple thought of defeating Drews. He was smashed by my forearm on a few occasions. Each time I landed one it sapped his energy — and his will to compete. I broke him, and I broke him early in the piece. The referee took exception to Drews's lack of fight and even stopped proceedings to order him to retaliate.

The crowd is crazed, willing me to the title. When I walked towards the ring they screamed and yelled and Hyder — 'H-man' — screamed in my ear: 'Can you feel the love, Greeny? Can you feel the love?' I could, and that love was there for each round. I hear the time-keeper crack a piece of wood on the canvas to signal that there is only 10 seconds remaining. I'm home and hosed. I feel an adrenaline overload and I raise my hands in victory. I had been critical of fighters for doing such things because I thought they'd exposed themselves to unnecessary danger by celebrating too early, but I don't care. I kiss the tattoo of my daughter Chloe on my bicep because I know she's watching the bout on television; I do a tumble turn and the bell sounds. The bout has ended. I've won the fight. I am world champion. I am so emotional I almost squeeze the life out of those in my corner because I hug them so tight. What a rush! People could never hope to appreciate the level of pain and torture it takes to get to this point. The sacrifice, the discipline and the dedication that is required for the privilege to wear the world champion's belt is incredible.

My thoughts turn to my heavily pregnant wife Nina. Our second child was meant to be born that night but she'd vowed to keep her 'legs crossed' to be ringside for the bout. I'm glad she's there because Nina inspires me. While the judges tally their cards I climb through the ropes and run towards her. I fight my way through the crowd and kiss her and then kiss her belly for our unborn child. I then move on to hug my father, my mother and my sisters. My brother Brendan (BG) is beside himself. In this magic moment our celebratory hug crushes some of the misery we shared from a family tragedy. The victory allowed us a moment to celebrate. In this magic moment it felt as if every hurt I've ever felt in my life has disappeared. There are no words to describe the electrifying feeling that's engulfed me ... it's a primal feeling that stems from being triumphant. On my return to the ring to hear the judge's decision I make it my mission to hug everyone to thank them for their support. I see the faces of the people who have been a part of the roller-coaster ride and they're all so happy for that belt to be wrapped around my waist. I hug Drews. He is a decent man.

Winning the world title was incredible, but the best was to come six days later when Nina gave birth to our second child, Archie Malcolm Green — 3.8 kilograms of love and hope. The 12-hour labour was tough. Nina was burning with a fever that should have made the mercury in the thermometer boil and the pain she endured made me cringe. The courage all women display to perform the miracle of birth puts men like me to shame. They go through hell, yet most back up to do it again. A boxer can stop fighting — if his will allows it — when he is hurt; a woman giving birth has nowhere to hide. Before I fought Drews I accepted that I might not be present at Archie's birth if he decided to enter the world the night before or on the day of the fight. As tough as I knew it would be I had to remain focused on beating Drews. Tough, but I was fighting for Archie's, Chloe's, Nina's and my future.

Before Archie was born I wondered how on earth I could love him as much as I do my daughter Chloe. She'd been my best little mate for five years and everything I did in life was with her best interests at heart. However, when he was born in the early hours of 22 December, I only needed to take one look to realise the human heart has an enormous capacity to expand and allow more love to enter it. I was so proud, and as I lay beside Nina with our baby boy I felt a great sense of worth and satisfaction. All was good in the world; and, believe me, it is very rare that a man who makes his living by fighting other men can feel that.

I am blessed.

I am champion of the world.

CHAPTER 2

THE HUMANITY OF BOXING

There is humanity in boxing. Believe me, I feel a deep empathy for the opponent I'm attempting to knock unconscious, but that's not obvious to the spectators who see only punches and blood. The humanity really kicks in after I've won a fight because even though I am not a religious person I offer a quick prayer that my opponent has finished the fight unscathed. I respect the fact he had the courage to get into the ring and put himself on the line because very few people do that in the course of their day at the office.

Throughout a fight I remain emotionless during a clinch or the split second after I've landed a heavy punch. I *must* ignore feeling empathy because boxing would be too hard if every boxer actually had to think about what they were doing to another human being. The only feelings you have for your rival is after a fight. Regardless of race, religion, colour or creed we've connected because he went through exactly what I went through during the fight: the fear of defeat, intense pain and the fact everything that mattered to him was on the line. By hurting — and defeating — him I have not only threatened that man's wellbeing but I've also risked his future earnings and his ability to make a living from the sport.

Kali Meehan, a Fijian-born, New Zealand-raised and Aussie-based heavyweight contender, says hate is not in his arsenal when he looks at his opponents: 'When I meet the other boxer people think I'm going to hate the opponent, but I don't. You know he's going through the same feelings and emotions you are and you connect that way.'

They're heavy-duty thoughts, and to dwell on them for too long can mess with your head because the one truth about boxing is a fighter gets rewarded for dominating and defeating his opponents; not pitying them. I *loved* winning and I *loved* fighting but to escape the complexities of boxing I spent time with my family; I'd go surfing or I'd play practical jokes on my mates. I'd also do things like throw bungers down at wannabe tough guys from the top storey of my base in Sydney when they'd scream out in the early hours of the morning and when I'd hide I'd laugh myself silly as they challenged the idiot who did that to show his face and face the music.

I did these things, even though they might appear immature to some, because I tried to not take myself too seriously whenever possible because as much as I loved boxing, it is a deadly serious business.

In the ring I constantly sneaked quick looks at my opponent's eyes because they aren't only the window to a man's soul, they're also a telling monitor of how he's holding up to being belted; to standing up to punches that would force most men to double over and cry out in pain. It's from reading his eyes after landing a heavy blow that I instinctively decided to unleash a KO punch or to remain patient and to continue to break him down and shatter his will. Either way, I learned it was important to remain emotionless — hot heart, cold head is how my Cuban-born trainer Ismael Salas described it. The best way to ensure I achieved that state of mind and maintained it in the heat of battle was to realise there is nothing personal about the fight. Even if my opponent insulted me in the lead up to a bout, well, I accepted that was just a part of the show for the public. History will tell you even the bloodiest of fights weren't won by insults. No, it's purely and simply business. To remain emotionless does not mean you are not passionate or determined to win, it simply means you stay in control when your every instinct has turned into electricity and *screams* for you to go wild. When my opponent's eyes revealed he was on the verge of going down, I had to either commit to the kill or defy the adrenaline rush and hold fire if he's in too awkward a position for a big punch to be effective. Whatever I decided, though, it was crucial it was properly executed. To lose my head and start thrashing wildly like I did as a raw amateur just because I had the scent of blood in my nostrils could've led to my downfall because it could have provided my opponent with an opportunity to throw a loaded punch that turned the tide of the bout in his favour.

Fighters such as Kostya Tszyu, one of the few undisputed champions of the modern era, have proven remaining cold and clinical is the best option. And while I strived to remain emotionless when my senses were 'wired' and focused on trying to floor my opponent, I learned I could still acknowledge he is my equal; that he not only bled red when he was cut but that he was doing exactly what I was trying to do: to survive and to finish the fight in triumph.

Some fighters believe the most humane way to deal with an opponent is to end the fight quickly by knocking him out. Joe Bugner, who locked horns with the likes of Muhammad Ali, Henry Cooper, Joe Frazier and Frank Bruno during an 83-fight career from 1967 to 1999, flattened men so as not to draw out their suffering.

'I personally do not go into the ring wanting to hurt anybody,' he said. 'I go in there to do a cold, calculated job and if I can beat the guy without hurting him that's great … but the only way I can do that is by knocking him stone cold.'

My twenty-fifth professional bout taught me it was to my advantage not to know the men I fought. Immediately following my loss to arch-rival Anthony Mundine I took on Jason 'The Nailer' DeLisle, a former world kickboxing champion who'd recently fought for the IBF world light heavyweight title, at Perth's Challenge Stadium. What made fighting Jason tough was the fact we are good mates. We don't see each other often but the mutual respect and admiration we feel for one another is strong; Jason says we are so close in our respective outlooks on life that we could quite easily be twins separated at birth. The fight was important to me on a number of fronts; I was returning to the ring from the loss to Mundine and I knew for the sake of my career my performance against Jason would be crucial because people were watching to see if I was 'damaged goods'. I *had* to beat Jason because a victory would also ensure I gained a top-15 world ranking by the IBF and WBA and that would — theoretically, at least — allow me the opportunity to try to avenge my opponent's ... my mate's... loss to England's world champion, Clinton Woods.

I thought the promise of a world ranking and ensuring Jason was both well paid and taken care of before — and after — the bout would help make my fighting him a little bit easier. However, while I pride myself on being the Green Machine and remaining emotionless when the referee orders me and my opponent to come out punching, this was the fight my 'game face' failed me because for the first time I started to think about the *man* I was boxing and what I was doing to him.

In my world-title bouts against the German Markus Beyer and the very tough Canadian Eric Lucas I switched off the emotion and embraced a hot head, cold heart. But that night against Jason I didn't just see an opponent, I saw a friend and it hurt to be hurting him. It was crazy. I cut Jason's forehead in the third round with a right and the wound later required ten stitches. As the fight progressed I closed one of his eyes and broke his nose. With each heavy hit seeming to hurt my mate I felt bad and despite having so much at stake there were times I found myself wishing his corner would throw in the towel to end the fight. Rather than continue to attack Jason's head as I would any other opponent, I targeted his body in the hope it would soften him up. However, in the eighth round he hit me plumb — it was a terrific shot — and it jolted me into action and I knuckled back down to business. After all, it was Jason who said in the prefight hype, 'It'll be him or me.' But as it turned out, the fight did end in the next round when his corner threw in the towel the instant I dropped him after a heavy five-punch combo. It was a relief to me in more ways than anyone watching on could have imagined. Jason might have had about ten people cheering him on in the crowd because he enjoyed a strong support base in Sydney, not Perth, but rightly or wrongly I doubt whether any of them felt for him quite like me. That's the humanity of boxing.

CHAPTER 3

GROWING PAINS

MY mum wouldn't have thought so at the time, I'm sure, but I consider myself lucky to have been an accident-prone child because breaking bones, grazing and bruising myself from a very young age allowed me to develop the pain threshold I needed as a professional boxer. While I remember a lot of kids at school would cry at the sight of their own blood, I devoured it. I never went out of my way to injure myself but I was the kid who'd find a way to somehow trip over a stone or a tree root. It must be in my genes because my cousin Brett McGuire is also injury prone.

I spent one Christmas in hospital after I crashed through a plate-glass window. When Jimmy Rickard and I raced on our bikes down the hill that started from our suburb of Doubleview and ended two kilometres away, by the surf at Scarborough, my front wheel hit a brick that was sticking out of the ground. I went over the handlebars, and I still wonder how the hell I didn't break my neck. It's funny, but when you're young those kinds of near misses don't register. If I remember correctly, my mate had a good laugh about my stack, and after I checked myself for any cuts or grazes we finished the race screaming and yahooing like banshees.

Even when I broke my collarbone playing footy, the sling my arm was put in didn't slow me down. One morning I chased my sister Sharni through the house and just as I caught up to her I slipped. I flew headfirst into a flower stand. A lump the size of Uluru formed on my melon. My leg also slammed into a side door and because I injured my knee it was hard to get back on my feet let alone walk. I wonder if other mothers took their kids to the local chemist after they'd injured themselves. Mum admits that when I smashed into the flower stand it looked as if I was a battered child. I had my arm in a sling, a monster egg growing out of my head and I needed a crutch to walk. The chemist took a look at my war wounds and after he handed me some pain-relief pills he suggested mum take me to the hospital for a doctor to look at me. To this day mum is embarrassed to admit there were quite a few suspicious looks trained on her as we left the store. For the record, I can say hand on heart that my siblings and I were blessed to not only have wonderful childhoods but also great parents who set the best examples for us.

My brother Brendan, better known as BG, was a bit too cool to have his baby brother hang around him when we were teenagers. I guess I may have been seen by him as a bit of a pest because I was like his shadow back then and tried to follow him everywhere. He was into his karate and footy, and was very popular. There were many fights — and tears —

between us before we became as close as we now are. BG is one of my most trusted mates who I seek out when I need advice. BG was in my corner during my fights and it was always a comfort to me to know he was there.

However, BG and I were pretty wild, and the odd crack with the old man's belt or the kettle chord and the occasional clip over the ear never went astray. A lot of people complain nowadays about parents physically disciplining their children. Times have changed and smacking your kids is frowned upon. While I prefer to discipline my daughter by making her miss out on something if she is naughty or rude, it's clear the old-school ways favoured by my dad weren't too bad. Crime rates are now through the roof, and respect for elders is severely lacking.

As a kid I always seemed to be close to the action and had a serious collection of grazes and scratches at the end of most days. Some of them were the result of fights. When I was 12 four of us decided to go to the local deli to buy some lollies after we'd spent hours catching frogs at the local swamp. An older kid, about 15, decided he'd pick a fight with one of my mates simply because he was unusually tall for his age. He cleared six foot in the old imperial measurements and even though my friend made it clear didn't want to fight, the older kid wouldn't let it go. My dad was my hero and I believed him when he'd told me bullies were only cowards who'd crumble if someone stood up to them. I fancied my chances and asked if he wanted to have a go. He did, but warned me he was a black belt in karate. He opened the fight by kicking me three times in my leg, but I didn't feel any pain because adrenaline was rushing through my body. I responded by throwing a few straight punches to his head and he crashed to the footpath and waved the white flag. It was a good victory and the Redskin lollies were on me as we watched the bully slink home. He never bothered us again but three days later my leg was painted an ugly purple and blue by the deep bruises that surfaced as a result of his going the boot. It was hard to walk but I didn't care; it was a badge of honour. I stick up for my mates, and they stick up for me.

Being the youngest kid of four meant I have always felt protected by my siblings. I can only imagine that is where the protective nature I feel for my family and friends stems from. I wouldn't hesitate to put myself on the line to shield them from anything. I am not only happy to live by that attitude, but I'm also proud to do so.

My two sisters, Narelle and Sharni, are an important part of my life. While things often keep us apart, the love I have for my sisters is important to me. I was so fortunate to have two loving and loyal older sisters who have looked out for me for as long as I can remember. They have supported me in all my endeavours, even my career choice — to get belted up for a living. If the truth be known, I probably inherited some of my fighter's instinct from my big sis 'Rel. I realised not to cross her long ago. Brendan forgot that golden rule when we entered a lift when we were kids on holiday. Five floors later the elevator door opened and BG came out with blood splattered all over his face and shirt. He was disrespectful and 'Rel gave him a good 'un. Narelle married Ken — or 'Jock', as the Scotsman is known in our household — and they've lived in the country for many years, which is right up Narelle's alley because she loves the laidback approach to life. The country suits her warm, animal-loving personality to a tee.

Unlike Narelle, Sharni copped a fair bit off me when I was a young punk. While we laugh about it now, I was constantly on her case, ribbing her and generally being a right little pest. Sharni was Chloe's schoolteacher and all the kids loved her. She cooks for me when I'm home and while she specialises in making all sorts of exotic, mad dishes for us, my favourite remains her eggs on toast; she does them perfectly. Anyone who knows me will tell you I am pedantic when it comes to my eggs. How two ratbags like BG and me ended up with such wonderful sisters I'll never know. Mind you, take the tip — if you wind up either of them they can handle themselves. I can't say enough nice things about my beautiful sisters, other than I have always — and always will — love and protect them. And stir them.

I have always been very close to my mum, Maria, or Ri-ri, as I call her. She has devoted her life to bringing us up in a loving and warm family home. I have always considered myself lucky to have her in our lives, and now that I have children of my own I appreciate her even more. Like Dad, Mum has always been there for us no matter what, and her greatest concern in life remains her kids and her grandkids. As a parent I now realise all the things she would nag me about were for my own good. But when you're young and stubborn, you don't dream that your mum could be making sense. More fool me. Mum, however, is no pushover and I guess that's because she had to deal with me, BG and Dad living under the same roof. I remember in the bad ol' days when BG and I would be in the kitchen having a fist fight over something stupid and Mum would ignore the punches to pull us apart. My wonderful mother has set a benchmark when it comes to love, warmth and class. It makes me very happy to be able to give her a big kiss and hug whenever I leave her house, and say: 'Love you, sweetheart'. Mum is just that — my sweetheart. These three beautiful women have had a massive impact on my life, and they've helped make me the person I am today. They may not realise it, but I love them deeply. It is my hope they each realise how much I love them.

CHAPTER 4

DUST UP AND DUST OFF

After I left school I gained an apprenticeship with the West Australian Water Board as a carpenter and I learned more about the older bloke's sense of humour than I did about 'dove tails' and other tricks of the chippies' trade. During my first few weeks on the job I was told to go and find such things as the 'wings' for the wing nuts, to buy a few tins of red-and-blue-striped paint from the hardware store and to find the sand for the sander. I was also told about the miracle of the blind carpenter who picked up a hammer and saw ... saw, as in see, get it? It was as funny as an uppercut to the guts but there was an even greater joke at the state government's expense. I was — at best — a very average carpenter's apprentice. I listened to my supervisor's advice, I could hammer the nails in straight and I'd saw through a piece of four-by-two without hacking chunks out of it. Miraculously, though, after my first year I was named the West Australian Water Board's Carpentry Apprentice of the

Year and it was a pretty big deal. A government minister, the top brass from the Water Board and a host of other bigwigs from the trade attended the awards night. I'm quite certain I wore a tie and when my boss spoke from behind the microphone I didn't hear any of the expletives that normally streamed from his mouth. The following year I won the award again and by the end of my apprenticeship I had defended my 'crown' for what I was told was a record fourth time. My résumé looked quite impressive and if my parents' pride was any gauge I figured four consecutive Water Board awards as best carpenter's apprentice would knock the socks off any prospective employer.

Suffice it to say, Mum and Dad weren't impressed when they learnt I was the only apprentice.

It wasn't all fun and games at the Water Board, though, because there was another apprentice — a tall, lanky electrician — who couldn't stand the sight of me and the feeling was mutual. We knew one another from school and even in the playground we rubbed each other up the wrong way for no reason in particular. The day we crossed paths at work I just knew the time would come when we'd go the knuckle, and it didn't take long for my prophecy to be realised … exactly three weeks. He fronted me in the car park one afternoon: 'Have you got a problem with me?' 'Yeah mate,' I snorted, accepting the challenge. 'I don't particularly like you!' He seemed shocked at my bluntness but once he'd collected his thoughts we agreed to sort out our differences. I told him get into his car and to follow me to a park not far from my house and the bloke promptly tailgated me *every* inch of the ten-kilometre drive, his stereo on full blast to pump himself up to heavy metal. '*Ha,*' *I thought*. '*This is going to be fun.*'

When we arrived at the park I took off my heavy work boots because they would have created some *serious* damage if I kicked the electrician with them. He did the same and to ensure no passersby could identify our employer we removed our shirts. Before we got started I was warned he knew karate and taekwondo and wouldn't be held responsible for whatever happened to me. I nodded, I understood and even though I shaped up I didn't want to be the one to throw the first punch because if there were any repercussions I figured there'd be some leniency if he started it.

I pushed him — hard — in the hope it would trigger an angry response but he merely shoved me back. I pushed him again and he responded with another push. It was handbags at 20 paces, and after about half a dozen pushes from both sides I shouted at him, 'MATE, I'M NOT THROWING THE FIRST PUNCH ... THROW SOMETHING! HAVE A FRIGGING GO, WHY DON'T YOU?' To help motivate him I grabbed the bloke by the throat hard and yelled into his face, 'C'MON, LET'S GO!'

Well, that fired him up! He went off like a firecracker. The apprentice 'sparky' went crazy and after a bloodcurdling scream he stepped back to set himself up for a punch or a kick (I can't remember what it was). I struck first with a big right to his head and knocked him out cold. It was a peach of a punch. His lip split like it was tissue paper and blood began spurting everywhere. I was worried I'd hit a vein and when I looked down at my hand I saw one of my knuckles was cut from having smacked his teeth. The scar is still there after all these years.

My greatest concern, however, was the fact he wasn't moving. My blood froze. 'Shit,' I thought, 'I've killed him … I've killed the bastard.' He was out for only ten or 20 seconds but it felt like an eternity. I helped him sit up and he was groggy. 'What happened? Who hit me? Where am I?'

He was still in Disneyland so I put him in the picture: 'Mate, I hit you. We were having a fight, I clocked you and you went down.' For a good five minutes he tried to piece the puzzle together. As for me I was clear-headed enough to realise our feud had to end in the park that day because I'd seen him out and about at parties and he hung out with what you might call a crew of 'likely lads' who weren't scared to cause trouble. I didn't want to be in the situation where I was on the wrong end of a 'back alley fair go' — three or four against one!

'Is that it, mate?' I asked. 'Are we done? Is this over?' I looked at him; he had a hole in his lip that was big enough for a train to run through. I figured the electrician would wave the white flag but boy, was I wrong. 'No, fuck no,' he slurred. 'Let's go. C'mon, let's go again.' Well, I had to admire his spark; the bastard at least had balls. 'Alright,' I said. 'No worries.' In the spirit of fair play I allowed him more time to recover. That, I figured, was the Aussie way. He finally climbed to his feet, dusted himself off and proceeded to stretch and limber up. The fight was again in him — I could deadset see fire burning in his eyes — 'YOU'RE FUCKED

NOW!' he screamed. I couldn't believe it, it was such a crazy situation, like a scene out of a Jean Claude van Damme movie and I couldn't help but laugh, collecting a kick to the head that caught me flush in the face and snapped me back into reality. I tripped and fell to the ground landing square on my arse. There was no mercy. He started kicking. Like a crab I scrambled backwards on my hands and feet and somehow evaded his kicks. 'You bastard,' I thought as I finally got to my feet. 'You tried to kick me when I was on the ground, you dog!' I was absolutely *filthy* and I landed a crisp jab to his head then followed that up by grabbing him in a headlock where I repeatedly smashed him in the face with some heavy uppercuts. I continued to smash him until he squealed for mercy and when he told me he'd had enough I landed one more blow for his trying to sink the boot in when I was on deck. He was a sight. His face was swollen, covered in blood, his lip was mashed up and I could tell by his eyes he was out of it again. The beating had left him delirious. I couldn't leave him in such a state at the park so I put him in my car, a '74 Gemini (my first motor) and drove towards the nearest medical centre for treatment. I was paranoid about losing my apprenticeship and thought my taking him to the doctor might assist in my defence *if* I was called up to explain what happened. Even though I'd thrown a towel over the passenger seat the poor bloke was bleeding like a stuck pig. I yelled at him to stop bleeding, but I may as well have told him not to blink or breathe, such was his state.

On the way to the doctor's surgery it struck me to stop off at my mate Benny O'Donnell's house because I figured he would find the situation amusing. When he opened the door of his house and saw me caked in blood Benny thought I'd killed someone. I opened the car door. The electrician almost fell out of the car and into the gutter.

'What the hell is going on, mate?' said Benny, alarmed.

'Remember him from school? We just had a punch-up and now I'm taking him to the doctor. I thought you'd get a laugh out of this.'

Benny had his giggle, I pushed the bloke's head back into the car and drove off towards the doctor's surgery. The poor woman behind the counter looked horrified when she saw me and 'my mate' walk through the door. We had no shirts or boots on, were both covered in blood and one of us looked half dead. She leapt from her chair and raced to get the doctor in what would've been Olympic medal-winning time.

When I was asked how my mate had come to look like this, I explained to the doctor we were playing football after work and I'd accidentally elbowed him in the face when I took a mark. I could tell by the look on the doc's face that he knew I was lying through my teeth. But the wound required extensive stitching inside and outside of his mouth and the doc wasn't able to do that at his surgery. 'Go to the hospital immediately,' he told me. By now I'd had enough. I figured I had beaten the electrician fair and square; I'd done my bit. There was no way in hell I was going to take him across town to the hospital. His father could deal with it. It's funny to think about it now, but on the way to his house we started talking. I asked again if our feud was over and he confirmed it was. 'Good,' I said, and to ensure he comprehended what had happened I added: 'I cracked you in the head, you kicked me in the face and I gave you a few to go on with. It's finished.' We didn't quite shake hands, but we could at least get on with our lives.

When I pulled into his street one of his mates was waiting for him in his front yard. I figured that would test our truce because he might decide to have a second go with some back-up, but the electrician proved true to his word. At the most I reckon our fight would have lasted no more than three minutes. But not only did I lose an hour trying to do the right thing but I would've driven about 30 kilometres after the fight to try and get his wound treated. A few days later when he was fit enough to return to work we actually parked our cars next to one another. There was no malice. We just nodded in acknowledgement and went on our way.

CHAPTER 5

PAT

Destiny smiled upon me the day in the early nineties when my dad taped a 'staff wanted' sign inside the front window of the new Hungry Jack's store he was to manage in the city. The following day a long line of job applicants stretched the full length of the block and around the corner. After interviewing heaps of people over six hours my father walked along the line and told the would-be applicants the interviews had finished for the day but they were welcome to return the following week. As the line dispersed Dad saw two blokes he thought looked like real 'goers' — blokes who *wanted* to work — so he took them aside for a quiet word and by the time their conversation ended Pat Devellerz and his brother Peter had second jobs to supplement the income they made for their families by working in a slaughterhouse. They didn't let Dad down because the brothers were great workers. Honest and trustworthy, they were always at the store on time and happy to work back late when Dad needed a hand. They clicked, and in time their relationship was not so much one of employer–employee, rather great mates who looked out for one another.

Before he migrated to Australia in the 1970s from Burma, Pat was a champion boxer. He represented Burma at the Asian Games in Thailand and won a silver medal at a tournament in the Philippines. Once in his new country, he didn't waste any time, training amateurs in his backyard, among the best of them his sons, Clyde, Rocky, Alfonze and Phillip. His daughter Annie probably saw more fights during her childhood than most boxing fans will in a lifetime! Pat, now in his 60s, has a little boy named Oscar and I'm certain he'll pull on the gloves at some stage of his life. Two things I can assure Oscar of is he not only has a great man as his father, but he has a brilliant trainer to one day teach him the craft.

When I found out Pat was a boxing trainer I tagged along with BG and Wizza to his gym in Koondoola one day. At that stage I'd had two amateur kickboxing fights (one win, one loss) and I was keen to fine-tune my punching technique. Brendan wanted to get fit for footy. After the first training session I was hooked. I always wanted to be a fighter and I felt Pat was the man to guide me.

He bears a striking resemblence to the late Japanese-American actor Pat Morita who starred as Mr Miyagi in the *Karate Kid* movies and it would crack me up when he'd unwittingly call me 'Daniel *san*' to emphasise a point.

I simply couldn't get enough of his training. I appreciated Pat's 'old school' approach. He demanded fitness and strength and he kept his instructions simple. He'd do things like buckle a belt around my waist that had a one-and-a-half-metre-long piece of rope attatched to an old car tyre. On his command I had to sprint 100 metres flat chat, and it was tough stuff. When I reached the point of what I thought was exhaustion Pat made me do it again ... and again ... and again. There was no respite, and to develop my upper body and torso I'd pick up a heavy sledgehammer and bash it into a tyre. Believe me, it was gut busting. My diet underwent a radical change too. I stopped eating cereal for breakfast and began eating raw steak and eggs.

A trainer is an important person to any boxer. He must be prepared to push a fighter when they don't want to train; he needs to be an amateur psychologist to punch the right buttons; he has to make hard calls and be honest when it might be easier to look away; he must develop a trust that can't be shaken and his ultimate responsibility is to look after the interests of his fighter at all costs. Pat fulfilled each criterion, working overtime on my jab — the bread-and-butter punch for any fighter — from day one. He helped hone it to such an extent I could knock opponents to the ground with a good, stiff left hand. He was such a good teacher. It was clear to anyone who watched him work that in his day he would have been a classy fighter. He was compact and quick and technically had it all. Just as importantly he had the ability to share his knowledge and wisdom. He could show a fighter how to throw a punch and why he shouldn't leave his head or ribs exposed. They say the best teachers are those who love their subject and Pat's passion and enthusiasm was infectious. He also was never scared to get close to the action and I remember one night when I accidentally whacked him in the face while we were doing some solid rounds on the pads and he started bleeding from his nose and lips. When I pulled up to apologise he just demanded I keep going: 'Lovely punch, keep punching!' He was a man who practised what he preached.

Pat's gym was by no stretch of the imagination luxurious; rough and ready would be a more appropriate description. Whenever it rained — or hailed — we would go through our punching drills under his carport — not that it offered much protection from the extremes because the rain would blow in from the sides and we'd still get drenched or stung by the hailstones. On those nights he'd have a steaming pot of Chinese tea close at hand to help pep us up. I loved the feeling of the two of us slugging it out, battling the elements.

Pat's troupe of fighters was like a gang of gypsies, always on the move training in different gymnasiums. One of our 'team' was John Steffensen, who later on in life won Olympic silver in the 4 x 400m athletics relay at Athens in 2004 and gold in the 400m at the Melbourne Commonwealth Games. I'm certain the tough nature of his training under Pat gave him a great advantage over his opponents on the running track because when Pat trained a boxer they had to dig deep.

It didn't matter which gym we visited, Pat was always greeted with great respect from the owner or manager and when he spoke influential people listened.

Today he's the boxing coach for the West Coast Eagles Australian Football League team (AFL) and I know the boys love and respect him the way I do. You cannot buy the experience he offers.

An important piece of Pat that was with me at every training session and it also accompanied me on my overseas campaigns — his old punching shield. It's sweat stained and I think it's the sweetest shield of its kind. Pat had it set aside as a family heirloom but he insisted I take it when I left Perth and apart from its practical purpose the shield holds special sentimental value for me. Every time I looked at it I was reminded of a man who taught me to train hard, punch hard and to fight hard.

CHAPTER 6

MIGHTY MARIST

Playing Aussie rules for the mighty Marist team in Perth's Claremont district competition from the under-9s to the under-17s taught me a number of valuable lessons that have stuck with me: you stand by your mates through thick and thin; a champion team will beat a team of champions; and persistence is rewarded.

Marist is still affiliated with my old school Newman College, but it wasn't run by the school. It's been a very successful little club thanks to the efforts of a lot of good parents who have worked hard to ensure it is well run and that the kids play for the right reasons. According to the club's records my brother Brendan, who was drafted into the West Coast Eagles Australian Football League's squad, is one of 22 Marist players who kicked on to play in the WAFL. Brendan played for Claremont and was a very talented rover who was renowned for being both very hard at the ball and hard headed. Marist also notes with justifiable pride that seven old boys have played in the AFL, including my old team-mates Matt Connell, who joined the Adelaide Crows, and Quentin Leach, of Fremantle Dockers fame — two top blokes who possess a great sense of humour.

I played my first game in the black and blue jumper when I was nine. I won a few trophies as our team's best and fairest in the early years but the best reward was that I made great mates — Justin 'Molly' Molinikos, Jimmy Tranter, Jimmy Rickard, Jezza, Heads, Benny, Odie, Davo and Macca. We went to school together, but the highlight of our week was undoubtedly Sunday morning when we played footy on the Northern Oval although for the first few years we were the competition's whipping boys. Lord knows we couldn't even buy a win back then because the other teams were too skilful for us. However, it said a lot for our team spirit that despite the losses we stuck it out together and had heaps of fun. My team-mates meant a lot to me. My father coached us while Molly's dad Lou was his assistant and the team manager. Rather than get caught up with the idea that we had to win, my dad, who was a talented bush footballer in his day, and Lou were more concerned that we simply competed, that we played fairly and everyone had a fair go. When we hit 14, the team clicked and we became the competition's pacesetters. We shone and it was reflected at the business end of the season when we won three grand finals. However, when I was 12 and Marist's fortunes started to dramatically improve, I stopped growing. It was tough because until then I had been a fairly big kid and played centre or rover. Despite my size, or rather lack of it, I was still quick and I used that zippiness to my advantage as a rover. I realised there was no point whingeing about my size because I couldn't make myself grow. Still, there were times when I wondered if I was ever going to catch up to the other blokes who towered over me.

I'm sure my team-mates would agree with me that our most memorable season was 1990 when we won the under-17 competition. It was a tough year because we were the team everyone wanted to beat. It was an even tougher winter for Molly because while we all loved him, our opponents picked on him because he was of Greek origin. They'd call him a 'wog' and target him for extra attention. To his credit I never saw Molly take a backwards step, and I well remember whenever there was a stink he'd be among the first in and he gave as good as he copped. These days, in between playing in a veterans competition, Justin helped promote my fights through Green Machine Promotions. Even in negotiating my bouts he was all heart. When things turned ugly at the end of the under-17 grand final Molly was in the thick of the action. Everyone expected West Coast (they have no affiliation with the AFL team, the Eagles) to win the title even though we'd played out of our skins the week before to defeat Carine, the side that was considered their strongest competition. The West Coast boys obviously thought very little of our chances because word filtered back to us that three days before the grand final they'd booked a hall to celebrate their victory. We used the image of them munching on party pies and drinking a sneaky celebratory beer as part of our motivation to beat them. Indeed, it's because of the lesson I learnt from the 1990 under-17s grand final that I refused to arrange a post-fight party, much to the annoyance of Molly and the other members of the Green Machine Promotions crew. They always wanted to arrange a get together for my sponsors and supporters, but I refused to be tempted to put the cart before the horse.

I will say that West Coast were a talented mob. Two of them went on to play in the AFL, Danny Southern for Footscray and David Sierakowski for St Kilda. However that didn't help their team that wild weekend in 1990 because mighty Marist was on fire. We couldn't put a foot wrong. But when the full-time hooter sounded we didn't get the chance to celebrate on the paddock because a brawl broke out when the West Coast ruckman attacked our ruckman Chris Headland. Because they were so tall and gangly, watching them slug it out was like watching two giraffes fighting on an African veldt. As I tried to wrench them apart the big fella threw a few wild ones my way. Brendan was our team runner and when he grabbed West Coast's ruckman in what was a genuine attempt to break up the fight, he didn't see me lining the bloke up for a shot. I was obscured by the ruckman's body because I was so short. It's funny, but even though I was only half the size of the other players I still packed a wallop and when I unleashed my big right hand just as Brendan grabbed the opposing player by his arms it landed straight on the button and the big bloke's knees buckled. I was then king hit from the side — and it was on for young and old, crowd and all. All I could see from my view on the ground was their boots the instant before they raked their studs over me. But my mates didn't abandon me; they flew straight into the action, punching, grappling and screaming. Unbeknown to the Marist boys, at the other end of the ground Molly was ambushed by two members of the Carine team who'd turned up to watch the grand final. They hurdled the fence and set upon him when the brawls erupted. One grabbed him in a bear-hug while the other laid into him. None of us helped him because we didn't see it; we were too caught up in the action with the West Coasters at our end of the field. But I guarantee you this, Molly would've given as good as he got. The ill feeling, like the dust, settled long ago. Occasionally I see some of those West Coast old boys around Perth, and while they don't ever seem too keen to dwell on that day the black and blues rained on their parade we do say g'day and have a laugh about it.

CHAPTER 7

FIRST BLOOD

Milos Radovich: the name is etched in my memory because in 1992 I came up against the bloke when I climbed through the ropes and into the boxing ring for the very first time. It was, as they say in the classics, my baptism of fire. Radovich, a heavily tattooed, goateed bruiser, was a few years older than me, and with a couple of his ten victories coming by way of knockout he'd gained a reputation around Perth's boxing gymnasiums as a KO puncher.

By contrast, I was just a skinny kid. On the surface it might have been a mismatch, but I was well trained and felt no great sense of trepidation because of the confidence my trainer Pat and the West Australian Boxing Association's Paddy Wilton had in me. After watching me spar Paddy said, 'You can beat Radovich.' Pat was also reassuring: 'No worries, Danny. It will be alright.'

'Sweet,' I thought, my heart pounding with excitement at the mere thought of the impending battle. 'There's no turning back!'

In our shared dressing-room at Midland Town Hall, a landmark building on the outskirts of Perth, I was hooked on the intensity of the build-up with Milos and I eyeing each other off like two wild dogs spoiling to fight over a scrap of meat. I watched Pat as he calmly went through what I had to do once the referee said to come out punching. The booming sound of other fighters punching their trainers' pads as they prepared for their date with destiny. The nervous energy of climbing up the three steps to enter the ring. Hearing my brother Brendan and my mates scream their words of encouragement from the back of the hall … it was a rush.

Anyone who says they don't feel fear going into a bout is a liar. There are various fears a fighter faces and the one that accompanied me into the ring that night as Milos tried to stare me down as the referee went through the rules was the fear of defeat. I dreaded what I imagined would be the sense of humiliation that would most certainly follow if I lost in front of my family and friends. Fear is present at all times in both corners of the boxing ring. However, a fighter's courage is being able to wrestle with that feeling and to control it. To do what is required to put up a good fight.

I stood in the opposite corner from Milos wearing a lime green singlet bearing a huge shamrock and the words IRISH FIGHT CLUB, a pair of baggy shorts and the old Converse boots I wore everywhere. Radovich wore slick boxing shorts and proper boxing boots — he looked the part. The first punch I copped was on the chin. A straight right. 'This is serious, mate,' I thought to myself, and it's funny to look back on it now but the idea he wanted to hurt me came as a shock.

I'd sparred plenty of rounds in the build-up to my debut, but I'd never before seen the look Milos had in his eyes: he looked like a shark that had tasted blood. But I stood my ground. I threw everything I had at him, catching him early with a one-two combination and as the seconds turned into minutes I was pleasantly surprised by how well I was handling myself. I remained calm and 'picked' my shots. In the third round I connected with a lovely one-two combination that wobbled him. I didn't need an invitation to get in amongst it. I let fly, my power coming from my boots, and in a frenzy I landed 15 unanswered blows. The ropes kept Milos on his feet and the referee had trouble prying me off him. His face was a bloody mess and the referee had no option but to stop the fight.

I think what I appreciated most of all that night was that the primal challenge of man against man is what fighters of all levels, be they world champions or nervous novices, crave when they pull on the gloves.

Defeat, however, can be hard for some warriors to accept. Milos was obviously unhappy with the result because he demanded a rematch. (I granted him his wish three years later when, in my eighth bout, I knocked him out early in the contest.) While that performance was a lot sharper than my 'first blood', I could never have imagined the incredible world that would open to me as a result of that debut bout at Midland Town Hall. I couldn't wipe the smile off my face for days; well, for two days to be precise, because that's when I was back at training with Pat and the hard work started all over again.

CHAPTER 8

RIDING THE THUNDER

Monster waves, and not monster fighters, scare the crap out of me. While most people think boxers are crazy, I reckon big-wave surfers carry the title of being the world's insanest athletes. They're the guys who chase 60-foot-plus waves and place their trust in themselves — and the great unknown — whenever they catch one. The energy and force they fight to ride that wave is incredible and I'm told being dumped by such a wave is like being trapped in a washing machine on the spin cycle. My mates and I surf in remote spots on the West Australian coast and while we push each other to challenge ourselves I'll take my chances in the ring — and against any man — ahead of such a wave.

I've surfed since I was 11, when I would paddle out to the waves off Scarborough on a 'foamie'. After three months it was replaced by a twin fin my father paid $95 for after days of scouring the classifieds in the local paper. Over the next four years I spent my summers chasing waves on that board and I became hooked on the adventure of surfing. Then I started riding a board that was shaped by Murray Smith, state surf champion in 1966 and one of the best shapers in the business. I bought a board from him that had been used by Dave McCauley, who at the peak of his career was the world's No. 2-ranked surfer, and it was a beauty. Dave rules one of my favourite waves down south, and he still blows everyone away when he is in the water.

There is an adrenaline rush when you catch a wave that makes it unlike any other feeling I know, but, as much as I hear some surfers talk about the 'spirituality' of the sport I haven't found that. Rather it is a great escape from life. As soon as I obtained my driver's licence it became my ticket to freedom. My mates and I would whack our boards on the roof of the car, throw our wetsuits and an esky into the boot and hotfoot it three hours' down south to chase that rush. We'd stay in old caravans that were covered in spider webs and contained horrible beds that you'd never dare sleep on. We lived mainly on a diet of baked beans, beer, laughs and sunsets. It was always fun and I loved nothing more than finishing a full day of surfing encrusted in salt and feeling bone tired. I've found surfing is an invaluable way to stay in touch with your mates. No matter how old we get or how full-on work and family commitments become a surf trip with mates is a great way to maintain those ties that bind us.

Many years after I went on my first surf safari, a 22-year-old bodyboarder named Matt Alford and his buddies hit the coastal highway, but his escapade turned into a genuine life and death battle when he was caught by what Yallingup's locals know as the undertow of a break called Rabbit's and sucked straight out to sea. After his wrist rope snapped and he lost his board, Matt was dumped by the swell, pinned to the sea floor, dragged towards land and then swept a few hundred metres away from the beach, the process was repeated over and over again.

That's where our destinies collided. My family and I had just finished visiting some friends at the local caravan park and were in the car ready to begin our long drive home when the park's manager bolted out of her office screaming that a bloke was drowning.

I hit the accelerator and practically flew the 150 metres to the beach and charged down the steps to see what needed to be done. While Matt was just a dot in the ocean, some 700 metres away, from where I stood it was obvious he was in distress — I could see he looked weak and, his body was limp. My immediate inclination was to dive in and swim to him but the surf was *thrashing* and I figured it would've taken me at least ten minutes, if not more, to reach him. I was worried he didn't have that much time — or fight — left in him so I bolted back to our car, hit the accelerator and fanged it towards my mate Johnsy's house. I charged up Johnsy's stairs, bashed on his door and yelled I was taking his surfboard from off the porch to save some poor bastard from drowning. Johnsy joined me and we drove as fast as we could back to the beach, where a crowd had gathered. He was hot on my heels as I sprinted the 400 metres down to the water.

I didn't have much time to think as I made my way into the ocean, but I was really scared I was going to see a man drown. The rescue was a bit like being in a fight because a million thoughts raced through my mind and the one that really rattled me was if I didn't succeed I would be retrieving a corpse. That made me push myself to go even faster and harder and I was screaming like a lunatic in the hope it would help Matt fight on: HANG ON, MATE! HANG ON, MAN! I'M COMING. HANG IN THERE!'

I lost sight of him momentarily when a wave swallowed him whole, but just when I thought he might not resurface his head popped up like a cork. When I eventually got to him I jumped off my board and Matt lifted himself aboard.

'Are you Danny Green?' he said, panting through exhaustion.

I didn't realise Matt was naked (he'd discarded his shorts and undies because they were dragging him under) until we were about 50 metres from shore and I gave him a push towards the shore. 'I just touched that guy's bare arse!' I thought to myself before I caught a wave and bodysurfed back to the beach. Back on land Matt collapsed to one knee. He was exhausted and just grateful to be alive and I was thankful to have been able to bring him back to shore breathing.

It didn't take long for word of the Yallingup rescue to get out and the wits (and believe me, there are plenty of them out there) didn't take long to nickname me 'Hoff', as in David Hasselhoff of *Baywatch* fame. Another of my mates superimposed my melon on Pamela Anderson's body and sent it around as an amusing email, and nowadays I won't be caught dead in red shorts.

I received a phone call from the Surf Lifesaving Association a few days later and was thanked for the successful rescue, but I'm certain I merely did what any strong swimmer would do in a similar circumstance. I was nominated for a bravery award, and while that was a great honour I think it should be noted on the weekend Matt Alford almost came to grief the lifesavers at my home beach, Scarborough, rescued 100 swimmers. However, their heroics barely rated a mention in the media. As far as I'm concerned the lifesavers and lifeguards are the genuine heroes because they're the men and women who go on beach patrol knowing they might be required to risk their lives to rescue a stranger. I just happened to be on the spot when Matt found himself in the wrong place.

CHAPTER 9

NINA

I first saw you when we were young, and even back then, I was completely stung.
Stung by a girl, who didn't know I was there, stung by a girl, with dyed red hair.
I asked her out, after months of courting, after months of anticipation, and mental sorting!
Then years later, our little gem was born, the girl that makes waking up fun, at the crack of dawn.
Plane trip to Vegas, then cab to the strip, three rounds later, Elvis let rip!
We were now one, after years of me and you and five years later, we've seen the crazy times through.
I love you, trust you, adore you, you're my star, I would be rich if I bottled your heart and sold it in a jar.
We've tasted good, bad, laughter and adversity. With my heart in your hands, I wish you Happy Fifth Anniversary.

— MY POEM TO NINA ON OUR FIFTH ANNIVERSARY

Words can't even begin to describe the love I feel for my wife, but on the eve of our fifth wedding anniversary in August 2007 I tried by putting my thoughts for Nina down on paper. I wrote it from the heart and while poems like this are normally a private declaration of love I'm happy to share it with the world because I'm so proud to call Nina my wife.

When a friend introduced me to Nina Cox 14 years ago it struck me she was quite beautiful. I'd actually met her four years earlier when she was only 16 and I was 17. She hung around with a different crew to mine but the reason I didn't attempt to even strike up a friendship with her was because I lacked the guts to say anything more than a jittery 'hi'. The first time we actually spoke was at a party and I was full of Dutch courage; unfortunately she was stone cold sober. I guessed the following morning that I'd made a goose of myself by trying to be witty when I was as smashed as a china plate at a Greek wedding. I reckon I must've called myself an 'idiot' a thousand times as I pieced together my grog-induced attempt to impress her. Thankfully there was one saving grace; I learned via the grapevine that Nina found my efforts to entertain her 'humorous'.

After that night I saw her at a few parties and while I tried to play it cool I was absolutely mesmerised by her. After a few conversations I finally built up the nerve to ask her out because I felt as if we got along well. The first film we saw together was the Quentin Tarantino movie *True Romance* where Christian Slater plays a bloke who marries a prostitute and then dreams Elvis visits him and says to kill the woman's pimp! Not the most romantic of choices, but I fell quickly in love with this girl and my days were soon consumed by thinking about her. It wasn't long before our friendship blossomed into something deeper.

I admired Nina's honesty and 13 years down the track, that hasn't changed. The secret to our happiness is the fact our relationship hasn't become complicated or stale. We love each other deeply and while my boxing career has been a roller-coaster ride with great highs and the occasional low, we've stuck it out together. She says living with me is like living on the edge, and fortunately for me Nina likes that.

Nina backed me to the hilt when I decided to move to the other side of the continent away from our family and friends so I could belt out a living as a professional boxer. When someone decides they are going to make their wage out of fighting there's no guarantee they can pay the rent, let alone the other bills needed for life's necessities. It takes a strong person to agree to such uncertainty, but Nina was not fazed at all. Her whole-hearted support was invaluable. She has been my backbone; my rock. Her faith in me means the world. She was well known in Perth as one of the state's top swimmers. Trained by 1968 Olympic gold medalist Lyn McClements she broke a number of Australian records and was selected in the national squad. Perhaps Nina's gift of knowing what to say and just as importantly when to say it stems back to her own experiences as a champion athlete.

As for my being a boxer she had no problem watching the fights even though she knew how tough it is. She doesn't like everything about the fight game, but she liked watching me box. Nina was well aware how hard I trained and prepared myself for my bouts so she knew I could handle whatever was thrown my way inside the ropes. The toughest part of my profession for her — and me — was the time we spent apart in the build up to a fight. The countdown to fight night is a tough time for any boxer, he's on edge and it doesn't take much for him to snap at a nothing comment. What is important in every day life takes a back seat to the business of boxing and winning. I found it was easier to move out of home and spare Nina and my loved ones from that side of the sport. It wasn't easy on her — or me for that matter –- but it had to be done.

We were married in Las Vegas in an Elvis Presley wedding chapel after I defeated Rhon Roberts of Guyana on the undercard of the Kostya Tszyu–Ben Tackie world title fight in May, 2002. We'd kept our decision to get married a closely guarded secret. The only people who knew we'd return from America as man and wife were our mothers. Nina's mother Liz was stoked to think we were getting married in a Presley chapel because she is a massive fan of the King's; she's adamant Elvis is still alive! My father, who was to be my best man, didn't even know about it until half an hour before we were to leave the hotel for the chapel. Dad was asleep when I burst into his room dressed as Elvis and when he opened his eyes the look on his face suggested he might've thought he was having a crazy dream when he saw me at the foot of this bed. He laughed off my declaration that Nina and I were getting married as another of my practical jokes. I had to get Nina to walk in the room in her wedding dress to prove I was serious.

For a long time my view on marriage was Nina and I didn't need a piece of paper to prove our love and commitment to one another. I knew she was the girl I'd spend the rest of my life with. Before Las Vegas we'd been together for seven great years; Chloe was four months old, and Nina is the most brilliant mother; we'd plotted numerous goals and shared our dreams; we'd travelled through Canada and in terms of my career Nina was always my backbone. I was fortunate that Nina appreciated I was on a mission to try to become the world champion when I moved to Sydney. She understood I needed to train, watch hours worth of fight tapes, that I needed to spend time with Jeff and the crew at the gym, I needed to go to sleep early and I had to follow a strict diet. Nina also realised my emotions would sometimes be a minefield because of the mood swings fighters go through.

It struck me to propose to Nina after I finished a tough training session in Sydney. As our home phone rang my guts churned with excitement; so typical of me to act on a spur of the moment thought, but it seemed perfectly right. When Nina answered the phone she was annoyed about something I'd done and tore into me. When she paused to draw a breath I asked if she'd marry me. She said 'yes' and proceeded to rip into me again before slamming the receiver down on me! *She hung up on me! I just proposed and she hung up the phone in my ear!* I phoned her straight back and we cracked up laughing. It might not sound as romantic as dropping a diamond ring in a glass of champagne, but the day Nina said 'yes' made me very proud.

Nina looked beautiful in her wedding dress and as we walked through the casino to the cheers and applause of well-wishers because I was decked out as Elvis. Dad walked 10 yards behind us shaking his head in disbelief at the latest 'adventure'. He thought we were crazy but in terms of marrying Nina I have never been surer of anything in my life. Our wedding was streamed live on the internet so our nearest and dearest could watch proceedings. I waved at the camera as I moon-walked up the aisle to the strains of Elvis singing *I Can't Help Falling in Love With You* and when I turned to Nina I knew, even from behind the massive Elvis-style sunglasses I was wearing, that I was very lucky to be marrying her. The minister, also dressed as Elvis, began the service with; '*Do you I'lle momma take this hunk-a-hunk of burning love to be you're wedded man?*' When we were pronounced man and wife the stereo was cranked up and Elvis' rendition of *Viva Las Vegas* filled through the room. Dad was dragged up — reluctantly — to dance as my 'I'lle momma' and I eventually shimmied our way out of the chapel happier than ever. Despite the stress of being married to a professional fighter, I like to think she believes the honeymoon hasn't ended. Because it hasn't for me …

CHAPTER 10

CHLOE

My hands have never let me down in the ring. Even when they've been broken and busted they have allowed me to finish what I started. However, my hands have never felt as strong and steady as in the early hours of 5 February 2002 when I cradled my newborn daughter, Chloe Elizabeth Green for the first time. They'd never held anything quite as precious before that morning. When Chloe was born at 11.58pm on 4 February she brought a light into our lives. I was rapt. I was thrilled by the idea of offering a child unconditional love, seeing the world through a kid's eyes and sharing her adventures — the good and bad. Fatherhood has been the most loving experience of my life — I've been blessed twice — and I've encouraged so many of my mates to go for it because everyone should experience the magic bond parents have with their children. The love I speak of gives me an extra reason to wake up each morning with a big smile on my face.

CHLOE

Nina didn't really need the pregnancy test soon after she arrived in Sydney from Perth because I not only had a premonition she was pregnant, but I knew we'd have a beautiful baby girl. For a long time Nina maintained that I was confident we'd have a daughter because it would mean I wouldn't be let down if we didn't have a son first up. That wasn't the case at all. My gut instinct was we'd have a little girl, and I couldn't have been happier. When we had Archie I was just as adamant we'd have a boy. I was out on a training run when Nina's pregnancy test confirmed my belief, and when it sunk in that I was about to become a dad it gave me an even greater reason to train harder at the gym and to win my fights to provide my family ... *my family* ... with some security. I was so happy it felt as if I was walking on air for a few days.

Two weeks before I was due to fight my eighth pro bout at Leichhardt against the Fijian warrior Iobe Ledua (on 8 February), Nina was 40 weeks pregnant. We went to the hospital on 29 January and the doctor said that unless Chloe was born beforehand he'd induce her birth on 8 February. That concerned me; not because it clashed with the date of my fight, but because I'd read that a 42-week gestation could be dangerous for both mother and child. I could hear the worry in my voice but the doctor didn't seem too bothered by my concerns. In the end I reacted by doing something that infuriated Nina — I wrapped my arm around his shoulder and squeezed tight as I said: 'Doc, I want you to come back to me with some good news. I don't want to miss the birth of my daughter (because of the fight) and I've read 42 weeks is unhealthy.' Come to think of it, lecturing a doctor about what was and was not dangerous was a bit rich, but I didn't care because all that mattered to me was the wellbeing of Nina and our baby. My leaning on him had its desired effect because a few minutes later the doctor returned and said: 'Good news, Mr Green. We'll induce your wife this Sunday.'

The doctor tried to induce the birth on the Sunday but Chloe must have been content where she was because it didn't work. The following day, after a five-hour labour, our darling daughter made her appearance. As soon as I saw her head I screamed at the top of my voice: 'She's got my ears!' It was an observation that didn't go down well with the midwife, who looked at me as if to tell me to shut up. But I wasn't joking; I was just so excited. I was warned in the lead-up to the biggest event of my life that many husbands fainted while they watched their wives give birth, but I was mesmerised by the miracle. It was the most beautiful, mind-blowing, natural rush ever. But there was a fright. The umbilical chord was wrapped around Chloe's throat, and she wasn't breathing properly. It took a good 30 seconds before she was given the all-clear. It seemed like an eternity. In my haste to meet my pride and joy I grabbed her from the doctor, wrapped her up, and sat down holding her. I was in a daze. I couldn't take my gaze away from the little miracle bundled in my arms. I was so proud. I stared into her eyes and introduced myself.

'I'm your dad, darling,' I gushed, fighting back tears of joy. 'I'm the person who has been talking to you for the last nine months. It's so good to see you at last.'

CHLOE

In my excited state, it took a few minutes before I realised Nina was waiting to give her daughter a loving hug. With Chloe resting between us that February morning, Nina and I shared an intense feeling of love and belonging; it was easily the greatest moment of our life together. Though we were blessed to experience that a second time with little Archie.

Nina's mum, Liz, stayed with us and was a massive help as we navigated our way through early parenthood. We appreciated her being about because it was also very reassuring to have someone on hand who knew not to rush to the doctors if Chloe coughed.

Nina reckons Chloe has me wrapped around her little finger, and she's spot on. My little girl won me over completely that first time I laid eyes on her because I immediately fell in love, and that feeling only gets stronger with each day. Nina gave me purpose to ensure I succeeded as a fighter. Chloe gave me an extra reason to ensure it worked. Archie has provided me with the will not to stuff things up.

Chloe can't possibly imagine the strength she instilled in me. One morning, when she was about 18 months old, I walked into her room and found her staring hard at one of my fight posters ... I mean really staring ... she looked at me and then fixed her eyes back on the poster. When I turned up to training that afternoon the memory of how she looked at that poster hit me hard and I thought that to give anything but my best in that session would not be fair to her. 'You're her world,' I thought. 'Don't you dare complain about being tired. Dig deeper, give more. You're fighting for her future now.'

I had Chloe's image tattooed on my left bicep — not only through fatherly pride but to re-enforce to myself why I'm fighting. There have been occasions when I've gained extra strength during a bout after I've sneaked a quick look at it. However, I didn't allow her to watch my fights when Chloe became old enough to understand what was going on and she didn't like it. It upset me greatly when I heard she'd cried whenever I was hit during my rematch with the German world champion Markus Beyer. She watched the bout on television while sitting on her aunt's lap, and I was told she had tears in her eyes for most of the 12 rounds. That's a lot for any kid to go through and I didn't want her to endure that. As her father I appreciated it was my job to protect Chloe from anything that might upset her, boxing included. Chloe's a sensitive, affectionate soul. She holds my hand tight whenever we go outside; she loves to cuddle and snuggle. Nina calls her my shadow because she's always hanging off me and it's funny but my little angel makes the most mundane of things great fun. The last thing she needed was to be upset by my job.

At age six, the world is opening up to Chloe and, like Nina, I'm seeing it through her eyes and it is a place of great beauty and wonder. I love the fact that when she played AFL in the mixed competition in Perth, Chloe was more interested in patting a stray dog than kicking the ball. She loves swimming, in the pool or the ocean, and she has inherited a few traits from me, including my sense of adventure. At the Sydney Royal Easter Show in 2007 she badgered me to go on a ride called the 'Slingshot' It is something I'd expect NASA's space program would put candidates through to see if they have the right stuff to become an astronaut. You basically sit in a seat and are catapulted 70 metres into the air at 165 kilometres an hour. I watched as fully grown men stepped off the ride with white faces and jelly legs, and had second thoughts about taking her on it. However, Chloe was insistent and I crumbled. What really horrified Nina and pleased me was that Chloe loved it. I know we're going to have lots of fun as she gets older and I know she's going to be a great big sister to Archie.

I don't think Chloe could possibly know how much her mother and I love her. She is everything to us, and the one promise I can make her is we'll always be there for her. The only expectations I have for Chloe — or Archie — is that they be courteous, compassionate, and be able to enjoy life. I would also like them to respect others and to stand up for the kids who can't fend for themselves because that was how my brother, sisters and I were raised. My simple wish is that they grow up to be happy and honest people with good values. Nina and I have been blessed.

FOR CHLOE AND ARCHIE

HEARTWARMERS

From the moment you were conceived you had my heart in a whirl,
Because deep down in my heart I knew you were a girl.
When you came into the world I felt we had already met,
And I had absolutely no idea how much joy I was going to get.
Then my little champ Archie made his grand appearance,
And now pride has my head so swollen that the doorway doesn't have enough clearance.
My gut told me a boy but I had no expectations,
And believe me it's true when I say this to you,
If you were a girl I'd make no renovations.

We have many cherished memories, Chloe, and so many more lie ahead,
I hope this warms your heart, little 'darl', that my favourite thing is tucking you into bed.
And as for you, my Tiger, we have a lot of living to do,
And just like your big sister I will always be there for you.
There for you when you are happy, there for you when you are sad,
There for you when you are excited, there for you when you are mad.
Beside you when you are winning, beside you if you are in strife,
My role as your father is simple — I'm here to protect you with my life.

CHAPTER 11

AMATEUR HOUR

In the countdown to the 2000 Olympic Games the Australian boxing team was a divided camp. There was a faction that did not want to train under East German Bodo Andreass, but I was not one among their number. While he was a tough taskmaster, I liked Bodo; I found him to be a decent bloke and a good coach. Regardless of my personal feelings about him, my view was he was the national coach and he deserved respect. Bodo was tremendous with such things as fitness, endurance training and, unlike his Aussie counterparts at the time, had a thorough understanding of the computer points system. Bodo did a lot to try and encourage a mind shift in the team. He taught us there was so much more to the sweet science than the brawling style we were renowned internationally for. The blokes with a set against Bodo, however, wanted to train under their own coaches in the final weeks before the Olympics, but you didn't have to be Einstein to realise that this was never going to happen. The rot had set in when the team flew to New Caledonia to train with the French, Italian and German Olympic teams. Some of the guys were worried about sparring against fighters who were considered serious medal contenders and refused to get in the ring. Morale was at rock bottom in New Caledonia and I was pissed off because it was having a negative impact on our Olympic campaign. The Europeans must have viewed the Aussie squad as an undisciplined rabble, and they were mostly right. One bloke took his washing to the local laundromat and we didn't see him for three days. I still have no idea where he went, what he did. It was crap. While I didn't get too involved in the politics of the team I did take one young bloke aside when it became obvious he was being influenced by a few strong-willed individuals and I advised him to pull his head in and just train. I was the voice of reason he needed to hear. While the blokes who were trying to get him on side to disrupt Bodo's preparation as they nursed 'injured' hands, the young fella jumped in the ring and dropped one of the Europeans who was considered a medal chance. That gave him extra confidence and when he stepped through the ropes at the end of his session I could see he was happy to have taken my tip.

When we returned to Australia word leaked to the media that all was not well in the team. Kostya Tszyu was brought in to help broker a peace deal between the factions and he was bewildered by what was going on. In the wash-up the authorities decided to sugarcoat what the real problem was and, in my opinion, instead made up rubbish like 'things fester, we got them off our chests and we are going forward' and 'the guys have all shook hands, we've spoken to the support people around us and we're all very positive'.

What a whitewash. The whole scenario opened my eyes to how issues and problems can be swept under the carpet to keep powerbrokers happy. And this was only boxing. Imagine the sort of manipulation that goes on in international politics. The bloke who made the most sense was James Swan, an indigenous Australian, who made an impassioned plea for calm: 'My dreaming spirit is the echidna and I use it to remind me of what I want to achieve. I am going to be so proud when I hang that gold medal around my little boy's neck.' I knew exactly where he was coming from because by the end of all the spin doctoring and other bullshit, I just wanted to whack on the gloves and box.

The politics didn't surprise me. I learnt amateur fighters are mere pawns when I qualified for the 2000 Oceania Games, which doubled as the Olympic trials for the Pacific Rim. I was advised at *midnight* on the Saturday night I *had* to contest a box off against Queensland's Kenny Dalton at 10am the following morning to secure my place in the national squad. I'd already fought on Wednesday, Friday and that Saturday. Jason DeLisle beat me by one lousy point in the final for the 'A' team and I took that on the chin. I was named in the Aussie 'B' team but the Queensland delegation weren't happy I made the cut ahead of their boy and petitioned for a rematch. The national body should have enforced its authority by saying their decision was final. However, I was informed by the West Australian team's management I had to be back in the ring at 10am Sunday. It was a joke, but I wasn't laughing…especially when I was informed I needed to be out of bed by 6am to make weight. Yeah, I spat the dummy but I eventually accepted the decision had nothing to do with my team management and I tried to get my head together to defend my berth. As you might imagine it was hard to fall asleep because I was terrified of sleeping in. I kept waking to see my alarm clock show it was 2.15am…3.12…4.47…5.00…5.23. My mind couldn't switch off because there was so much at stake.

I knew my chance of making the Olympic team was on the line as Dalton established a points lead after the opening two rounds. In between the rounds I not only eyed off those who made me fight but I also mouthed obscenities at them. It was pointless and it was immature, but I was absolutely filthy on the system. I was paying a price on the scorecards because of my anger, but I managed to knuckle down — literally — the third and fourth rounds when it was rammed home that I was allowing an opportunity to become an Olympian slip through my fingers. I knocked Dalton out in the fourth and final round. I wasn't angry at Kenny — he was simply doing his best — but I was filthy to think I was put through such an ordeal. Dad and Brendan were at the fight and after making the Olympic qualification tournament on the back of an emphatic KO I couldn't wipe the smile off my face or get a full beer out of my hand that entire afternoon. I went to the Oceania tournament and gained my Olympic berth when I won the gold medal for knocking out the Tongan who defeated Jason DeLisle.

The Sydney Olympics was to be my last hurrah as an amateur. I'd made the decision to turn professional during my final training session at Jeff Fenech's gym in Sydney where I sparred with the likes of Glen Kelly who went on to fight Roy Jones Jnr for the world title. The Olympics would become one of the highlights of my life. Even though Australia had a record ten fighters qualify — Paul Miller, Henry Collins, Daniel Geale, Justin Kane, Michael Katsidis, Brad Hore, Richard Rowles, myself, James Swan and Erle Wiltshire — the odds were stacked against us getting through to the medal round. None of us lacked ticker, but we were up against it when the likes of America spent a reported $US3 million on their boxing team.

The amateur boxing officials, obviously aware there would be questions asked about our performances, were on the defensive before we even threw a punch in anger. Arthur Tunstall, the el supremo of the amateur movement in NSW, blamed the team's gloomy prospects on the lack of sponsorship dollars. The Australian Medical Association's constant harping on the perceived dangers of the sport were a turnoff for would-be sponsors, he said. While there might be an element of truth to that, it is my belief that amateur boxing has far bigger problems such as infighting, petty jealousies, lack of promotion, lack of regulation has hindered the sport's progress. It's a pity because our amateur boxers need a profile; they need for the public to recognise their efforts.

On 15 September 2000 I was among the 600-odd members of the Australian Olympic team milling outside the newly constructed Superdome complex at Sydney's Homebush Bay and I was buzzing. As host country we were the last of 199 nations to enter the arena so we waited ... and waited ... *and waited* while the other teams savoured the applause and goodwill of 110,000 spectators. A few of the boxers and I passed the time by chewing the fat with Cathy Freeman and super motivator Laurie Lawrence. Laurie was pumped that night, but I have a feeling he's like that all the time.

Many statements were made that night: North and South Korea embraced the spirit of the Olympic movement to use sport as a vehicle to promote world peace by marching under the one flag. Four athletes from East Timor, which had only recently gained its independence from Indonesia, received a massive ovation when they marched beneath the IOC's banner. Then there was my own.

As the time drew closer for us to walk into the arena I snuck off to the men's room to paint my face green and gold with zinc cream. The reason was twofold — my sense of patriotism but also to get my melon on television so my family and friends back in Perth could see me enter sport's greatest stage. I knew the cameras wouldn't zoom in on an obscure boxer because they'd be too busy scoping the household names: Susie O'Neill, Cathy Freeman, Kieren Perkins and Ian Thorpe. Bearing that in mind I decided to give them something they couldn't possibly ignore — a green 'n' gold nutter! When I rejoined the throng from my art session, plenty of athletes looked at me and said, 'What a great idea, I wish I had've thought of that' but I was glad they didn't; this was one occasion when I wanted to stand out from the crowd.

At the first sight of the Australian flag the crowd went wild. The din was deafening. A rolling ocean of Aussie flags swept around the stadium. I didn't cry, but I had goosebumps all over and there was certainly a lump in my throat. The experience was quite humbling. I kept saying to my good mate Paul 'Mr Magic' Miller, 'Can you believe this?' just to make sure it wasn't a dream. Each member of the team was handed toy boxing kangaroos to throw into the crowd but in my excited state I was absolutely *hurling* them. I hope I didn't hurt anyone. I was so excited I ran up to a Channel Seven cameraman, looked down the barrel and screamed, 'YEEEOWWW! HELLO PERTH! WESTERN AUSTRALIA! I LOVE YOU! Needless to say the sight of me yahooing and playing the goat on the other side of the continent amused the Green household no end.

After my impromptu performance on national television I saw Pat in the crowd and broke ranks to give my first coach an almighty hug. My Olympic selection was as much an achievement for him as it was me so it was special to be able to share that moment with him. After all those training sessions in his carport, putting up with a temperamental fighter, sacrificing time with his family, putting his faith in my ability and character it made me so proud to know he was there with me at the Olympics. That hug was a story in itself. If I could have I would have placed Pat on my shoulders and carried him around the arena for the rest of the ceremony. He deserved it.

No-one really expected us Aussie boxers to strike a blow against Cuba, USA, Russia and the other European nations

— 'outside medal chance' was the best rap any of our fighters received — yet, standing in the Olympic Stadium that night I vowed to spill as much of my own blood as was necessary and to endure whatever pain required not to let my country down.

CHAPTER 12

MEETING ALI

If I did nothing else at the Sydney Olympics I made an impact on the great Muhammad Ali. Unfortunately it wasn't for my punching power or even my athletic prowess, instead the hero of the 'Rumble of the Jungle' and other epic battles including his shock win over Sonny Liston in 1964 will perhaps remember me because of an unfortunate slip of my tongue which shocked him and embarrassed the tripe out of me.

Young or old, black or white it's every fighter's dream to meet Ali, and I was no different. I regard him as the greatest boxer of all time and, more importantly, he's a fine person who has dedicated his life to drawing the world's attention to poverty, starvation, illiteracy and injustice. Many athletes have tried to emulate Ali's deeds in and out of the sports arena, but none have touched hearts quite like him.

I was in the Athlete's Village sound asleep when one of the boys charged into my room at about 9am screaming at the top of his voice, 'GREENY! GET UP! MUHAMMAD ALI IS

IN THE FOOD HALL!' I was out of bed so quickly you would have thought the place was on fire! I hit the floor running; there was no way I was going to miss my chance to shake hands with one of the few athletes I consider a hero. I flew out the door only to realise I was still dressed in the boxer shorts and old T-shirt I'd slept in. I ran back inside and put on my team strip and started to sprint the 750 metres from my room to the dining hall only to realise I'd left my camera on my dressing table. My quest to meet Ali was turning into an extra training session!

But the sight that ultimately greeted me when I got there was heartbreaking. A mob, it must have been at least 1000-strong, surrounded Ali. Like me they all wanted to shake his hand and to get their photograph taken with him. I didn't know what to do, join the herd or go back to bed when two members of the NSW Special Police Group (SPG) asked me what was wrong. (Being a sociable group boxers would sit on our verandah during the day and try to chat to passersby, including the SPG boys. The athletes from the other sports weren't as keen for idle talk as we were.)

'I'm spewing Look at the line, I won't get to meet him,' I said.

I swear I wasn't in any way wanting them to use their influence to help me meet Ali but they took matters into their own hands.

'Come with me, mate,' said one of the wallopers. 'If an Aussie boxer can't meet Ali, *no-one* will.'

With that the boys plonked me fourth from the front of the queue. It was the only time in my life I've ever jumped the line and, boy, I felt low. I wanted to crawl under a rock because I could feel hundreds — *and I mean hundreds* — of angry eyes drilling holes into the back of my head. All I could do was pull my cap down over my eyes to hide both my face and embarrassment.

Within seconds of me taking my place Ali's minder told the poor guy behind me Ali would leave after *I* met him. I think he might have been a German pole vaulter and he was pissed off, and rightly so. I could hear more groans of disappointment further down the line when someone said over the public announcement system, 'No more people today. Come back tomorrow.' I knew there was no hope in hell Ali would return, but I thought the organisers were smart to say that because there would have been a riot otherwise, everyone was so desperate to get up close and personal with the self-proclaimed Black Superman.

Ali wore sunglasses as he posed for photos and listened to athletes say what an inspiration he had been to them but when he was told I was a boxer from Australia he took off his glasses, looked me square in the eye and shook my hand. He put his fist up to me, as he had done to everyone else, for the camera but rather than raise my hand I wrapped my arm around his shoulder. He didn't speak but Ali pointed to my fist and then to his lips. I had no idea what he meant. My initial thought was he was telling me to keep quiet, but then it dawned on me he was asking me to put my fist to his chin. 'No way Muhammad, you're the greatest, I can't do that,' I said. I kept my arm around his shoulder and the photo is priceless, it's something I am very proud of.

My minute with the legend went far too quickly and as I stood to leave he muttered something like 'Go get 'em champ' or 'All the best' and I was walking on air. There was so much I could have said to him but in my excited state I tapped him on the shoulder and yelled, 'MATE, YOU ARE THE FUCKING GREATEST!' When I realised what I'd said I wanted the ground to open up and swallow me whole. I went crimson with embarrassment and tried to slink away, but Ali was looking at me and I remember the glint in his eye — it was a warm and mischievous one, as if he was thinking 'That cheeky little bugger just swore at me!' That look put my mind at ease. And it's a memory that will last forever.

CHAPTER 13

THE BOY FROM BRAZIL

With an uneasy truce finally brokered the members of the Australian boxing team focused on the job we'd been selected for: to fight, and to represent our country with pride. I didn't fall asleep until 4am of the day I was scheduled to fight Brazil's Laudelino Jose Barros, a silver medalist at the 1999 Pan America Games, due to a combination of nerves and the rush of excitement from watching Paul Miller win his first-round fight against Jerson Ravelo, a 'banger' from the Dominican Republic. I watched the bout on the television set in the common room of our quarters at the Athlete's Village and it was a typical gutsy Miller performance. The Queenslander was 'wobbled' in the second round by a heavy blow that should have knocked him out cold, but Paul has always fought with a 'no retreat, no surrender' attitude and, as Ravelo discovered, it's hard to beat someone who possesses those qualities. 'Paul underlined his toughness when he entered the 2000 Oceania Championships with a cracked rib, a foot injury and a hand problem that required surgery straight after the championships. Yet, despite those handicaps, he won the gold and secured his place in the Olympic team. Once he recovered from Ravelo's heavy punch Paul fought back strongly and skilfully to win by a point, a decision, which angered his opponent. He was simply outboxed in a very close fight.

When Paul returned to Homebush he was on a high and we spoke for hours. It wasn't until I relived his fight punch by punch that I turned in. But I couldn't sleep; the challenge that waited that evening of 20 September made it very hard to switch off. I received an almighty boost when I saw Nina, Dad, BG and the gang after being away from Perth for so long. The support put everything into perspective — I wanted to win for them.

As soon as I entered halls 3 and 4 of the Darling Harbour Exhibition Centre, the boxing venue for the Games, I was jolted by the electric atmosphere. It was packed to the rafters. The likes of Muhammad Ali, Evander Holyfield and other boxing greats were ringside throughout the tournament and the parochial Aussie crowd made it a very special place for one of their countrymen to box in. Because of the Olympic fever gripping Sydney, the demand for tickets far outweighed the supply so your typical footy- and cricket-obsessed Aussie sports fan was clamouring to watch sports they'd never before contemplated attending. The night I made my appearance in the Olympic 'cauldron' the crowd was aware an Aussie was involved in the last bout of the card and, boy, they were primed for it. We were invited to pick a song to have played as we marched to the ring. A lot of the blokes picked rap songs which failed to strike a chord with the audience. Me? I chose Men at Work's 'Down Under'. When the few first strains of the song were played over the PA most of the 8000-strong crowd went absolutely nuts.

I floated all the way to the ring because the crowd's response to an Aussie fighting and to the song's lines about being handed a 'Vegemite sandwich by a man in Brussels' and 'I come from the land of plenty' was sen-bloody-sational. It took a world title fight in Perth to match that reception and it sparked an intense will to perform for the crowd. Pity poor old Barros I was ready to take on the world, let alone a 24-year-old from Sao Paulo. But he didn't need a second invitation to rip into me once the fight started. Ours was an old fashioned slugfest, and the crowd lapped it up. Unlike most of the other fights that night, which were deft displays of technique and finesse, ours was what Australian sports fans appreciate most — plenty of claret. The South American was like the proverbial thrashing machine but I always felt in control. The referee, eventually, stopped proceedings in the fourth round when I had gained an insurmountable points lead after dropping him with a right to the chin. When I raised my fist in victory, I was so pumped I didn't even smile. I was so overwhelmed with pride and a sense of achievement that I found it hard to breathe. I'd won gold medals at the Oceania and Arafura Games, bronze at the prestigious Liverpool Cup in England and the Mayors Cup in Philippines, but nothing up to that point matched my victory over the Brazilian. You see, Aussies don't normally win fights at the Olympics and my progressing through to the second round was a real breakthrough. My team-mates — Paul Miller, Justin Cane and Michael Katsidis — also experienced the massive boost of winning their first bout. It was a great lift, too, for Australian amateur boxing to finally see some positive headlines about our team rather than the negative crap that plagued our build-up.

CHAPTER 14

THE BEAST FROM THE EAST

My celebrations were short-lived. When the draw for the 81kg division was announced I learned I was in for a torrid time. My opponent was Aleksandra Lebziak, at that time, one of the best pound-for-pound amateur boxers in the world. Yet I wasn't fazed in the slightest.

If I was certain of anything about my Olympic campaign it was at some stage of the tournament I'd lock horns with Lebziak. Along with Cuba's heavyweight Felix Savon, Lebziak was perhaps the best credentialled boxer in Sydney. Apart from winning a world championship crown in 1997 he was known in Australian fight circles for putting Justann Crawford in hospital during the 1996 Atlanta Games. During a wild exchange he cracked Justann behind the head and the Aussie warrior appeared to be in serious strife when the medicos scrambled to treat him. There aren't many people who are as tough as Justann and my mate could definitely handle himself in the ring, but made a full recovery and while he did not box at Sydney he was on deck as a volunteer to help spectators get all they possibly could from their Olympic experience. A few days before the boxing competition started Justann and I joked about me squaring the ledger for Atlanta, but I 'touched wood' — as is my superstition. *I* didn't want to jinx myself and be hospitalised like my mate.

I wasn't apprehensive; I wanted to test myself, to see how I went against the best, of the best, but I was wary. Lebziak had monstered an extremely tall boxer from Senegal in his opening bout like a lion taking down a giraffe. But the pressure was on *him*. After all, Lebziak was the overwhelming favourite and as the underdog I had nothing to lose.

On the night of the fight, I caught one of the shuttle buses that ferried athletes from the Athlete's Village to Darling Harbour. It was dark when I climbed aboard alone and it took me a few seconds to realise the only other people on the bus were Lebziak and his trainers! My instinctive reaction to seeing my opponent sitting there was to plonk myself on the seat immediately in front of him. Nice and close to let him know I didn't give a damn. I put my headphones on and tuned out, but there was a problem. I'd picked up a bad cough the previous day and for the entire trip I had to suppress my desire to cough because I didn't want Lebziak to gain a psychological advantage by thinking I was crook.

In the warm-up area Lebziak, an officer in the Russian army, hit the pads so hard it sounded as though he was detonating bombs. BOOM! BOOM! BOOM! Bodo Andreass had prepared page upon page of tactics for me to digest but as I gloved up I informed Bodo to put his plan away because I intended to fight the bout on my terms. We were going to see how Lebziak handled himself.

When the time came to face the music I again marched into the ring to 'Down Under' and the crowd erupted. Again, I fed off their response and promised myself to give them something to really cheer once the action started. When I climbed through the ropes and stood before Lebziak, however, I knew I was looking into the eyes of a true warrior. His face not only bore the scars of his 300-odd bouts, but he was supremely confident. He had every reason to feel smug. After all, who was I to him? I made it my mission to at least knock that look from his face and to the crazed cheers of the parochial crowd I unloaded a pearl of a punch square on his cheek early on. The blow *should* have depressed Lebziak's cheekbone but his head was as hard as granite and a sharp pain shot straight up my arm the moment my fist connected with it. Having previously broken hands in the ring I knew all too well I'd busted my mitt. But despite the handicap I continued serving it up to him and returned to my corner with a 3-2 lead. I was stoked to have had the better of the round but there was also an element of disappointment because when you fight someone of Lebziak's calibre you need *four* healthy hands, not one.

My corner, Bodo especially, was ecstatic because I'd taken the fight to the Russian and struck a blow in more ways than one. But I was reluctant to let anyone know my hand was 'gone' because there were television cameras and microphones in our faces. I was worried if I piped up news of my injury would somehow reach the ringside doctor and the fight would be stopped. It wasn't until the last few seconds before I returned to the ring that I confided in Bodo and all he could do was tap me on the hip as a show of sympathy; the disappointment was obvious in his eyes.

However, I didn't return to the battle feeling as if I was a beaten man. I still believed I could win; it had just become a bit tougher and that feeling was only galvanised when I threw a left hook that sent the world champion crashing to the canvas. It was mad. I was hoping he wouldn't get back up; the crowd erupted and the chant of 'Aussie! Aussie! Aussie! Oi! Oi! Oi!' was so loud it threatened to lift the roof off the Exhibition Centre. My mates Brooksy and Wizza went absolutely nuts and later when I watched the tape of the fight I laughed myself silly at the sight of Wizza hugging Laurie Lawrence.

Humbled by his tumble Lebziak launched a series of savage raids, but I pressed on. I was so psyched from landing that hook I had *yet* another crack at his head with my broken right, but it was a bad call: the pain shot up my arm again, but my determination to do Australia proud ensured I kept swinging. There was no way I was going to raise the white flag. As I withstood bombardment after bombardment I yelled to myself, 'What is the worst thing that can happen here, mate?' Getting stretchered out? Big fucking deal! Get in there and keep fucking fighting!' With that I'd throw another punch and repel his raids by jabbing out my left hand like a spear. Amazingly by the end of the second round I'd compiled a 5–3 lead and my corner was rapt. Like me they hoped against all hope that I could pull off a massive upset. After all I'd dropped Lebziak; I'd landed some good blows and despite a badly busted hand I was still standing. But the Russian had something else in store.

In the third round he broke my nose with a wicked shot and blood spurted from my hooter as if it was a fountain. When the ringside doctor suggested the bout should be stopped I lost the plot; I yelled for him to 'fuck off' as there was no way I was going to allow him to end it. I even banged on my nose to prove the pain was insignificant. Shit, I'd danced about for the better part of three rounds with a broken hand, so what was a busted nose? I'd had plenty before. 'What have I got to lose?' I screamed. The doctor relented and allowed the fight to continue, but despite more protests the referee soon called it to a halt to enforce the amateur rule that a fight must end when the dominant boxer gains a 15-point lead.

While I was bitterly disappointed I was moved by the respect Lebziak afforded me after the bout when he commended me for what he called a great effort. The crowd also floored me. They gave me a standing ovation as a show of their appreciation. I took their reception as a sign I hadn't let Australia down and upon realising that I became very emotional. So, too, did the people who mattered most to me: Dad, Mum, Nina, BG, Sharni, Narelle, Jules and the gang including Wizza, Molly and Brooksy.

That Lebziak fight was my last as an amateur and the Russian would go on to cut a swathe through the light-heavyweight division to finish as gold medallist. He was a deserved champion and when we met later in the Games I was pleased to learn Aleksandra was not the stereotypical harsh East European you see portrayed in most Hollywood films. He was the opposite: a warm-hearted bloke blessed with a good sense of humour who made it clear he wouldn't forget our fight in a hurry. I'm only sorry I didn't get a crack at him in the professional ranks because he retired in 2001 after winning his only pro fight by KO over an American journeyman named Stacy Goodson. I might not have won an Olympic medal at Sydney but I still have the red shorts I fought Lebziak in. They're stained with our blood and when I look at them and think of the challenge I faced that night I can't help but feel very proud.

CHAPTER 15

BEATEN BY A NOSE

While I've had a few hairy experiences in the ring during my career, the only time I've ever felt *real* terror was in a toilet at Sydney airport in 1998 when I thought a piece of my brain had fallen out of my nose. I'd just returned from an international tournament in the Philippines where I knocked a Korean out cold, but in my next fight I was on the receiving end of a German slugger's thunderous left hook which just about tore my nose from my face. The blow staggered me but I didn't go down. The referee stopped the bout and applied a standing count. When he reached eight I put my hands up to show him I was fine to continue but it was at that very moment blood gushed from my nostrils like a burst water main. The referee asked if I could continue and I nodded, 'Yep, bring it on.' However, when I shaped up to the German something obstructed the vision from out of my left eye and after a few seconds it dawned on me my nose had been driven so far over to the left-hand side of my face it was actually blocking my sight.

The German and I traded a few more punches but because my blood was pouring everywhere the referee intervened and stopped the bout and allowed the ringside doctor to take a look at my beak. I noticed the doctor actually grimaced when he observed the full extent of my injury and he put an immediate end to the fight. My team-mates all looked at me in absolute horror after I left the ring: 'Oh, no, Greeny, look at your nose!' All I could say when I looked in the dressing-room mirror was 'Holy hell! This looks terrible!' I urged the Aussie team manager to put my nose back in place, but he turned white. 'I can't,' he said, recoiling in horror. 'I just can't.'

'Just do it. Get a towel and pop it over. Do it now before it gets too hard.' But he wouldn't budge and insisted I go to hospital.

Going to the local emergency ward worried me a heck of a lot more than the actual injury because we were on Bocolod, a remote island in the archipelago. But I had no choice, no-one in the dressing room wanted to set my nose, so I climbed into the back of an ambulance accompanied by a team-mate and the manager. My boxing gear was caked in blood and as the ambulance raced through the streets with its siren wailing I felt a sense of dread for what awaited me. I'd heard horror stories about Asian hospitals: people going in for stitches and leaving with gangrene, that sort of thing, and when we arrived the doctor on duty refused point blank to touch my nose. He said they would call in their ear, throat and nose

(ENT) specialist and I was stunned because I doubt if you would even get that kind of treatment in Australia.

'What kind of specialist are they going to have here in Bocolod?' I asked.

Thankfully, the doctor wasn't offended by either the tone in my voice or the question. He instead told me not to worry because the specialist would be there in 50 minutes.

There were no beds available so the ENT led me into a storage room. I thought my worst fears were about to be realised when he sat me down on a chair and had my team-mates hold me down by one side while the team manager weighed down my other side. Within a matter of seconds he'd injected a total of eight needles in my nose — four of which went up inside each nostril — to anaesthetise the area before he set it back into place. The needles were as thick as matchsticks, so as you might imagine it wasn't an enjoyable experience. The doctor then grabbed my face and started to push my nose back into place. I pride myself on having a high pain threshold but the pain shooting from my nose was so intense it felt as if he was tearing my brain apart. I yelled for him to stop and when he asked if I could feel 'it' I couldn't control my tongue and yelled, 'OF COURSE I CAN FUCKING FEEL IT! FUCK THIS, MATE!' He wasn't in the slightest bit fazed. He simply stopped what he was doing, grabbed another needle and injected yet *another* eight needles in my nose — that made 16 jabs in all — and then said calmly, 'Right, quick. You will hear crunching, but don't worry.'

Blood pissed out of my nose and tears filled my eyes while the ENT grabbed a pair of foreceps and stuffed what felt like

2 metres' worth of gauze up each nostril. To this day I still have no idea where it all went. And, that was it; he told me under no circumstance was I to sneeze, cough or blow my nose … and after saying he'd see me in two days I was sent on my way.

I returned to the hospital two days later and was warned once he started to remove the gauze from my nose that it would *hurt*. He was right. I was in agony. The floor of the examination room was literally awash with blood. But after he'd removed all the gauze he produced a spray and squirted it up each nostril and the bleeding stopped immediately. It was incredible. When he asked me if I could breathe through my nose I took a deep breath and was pleasantly surprised to realise he'd fixed me up; it was actually the best my nose had felt in years

Two days later I was in the men's room at Sydney airport and as I washed my hands the ENT's warning for me not to sneeze, cough or blow my nose too hard rang in my ears as I felt an itch inside it. I blew my nose, as instructed, gently and this *thing* emptied from my left nostril. It was like a piece of pear but the size of a lipstick container and it was covered in a mess of blood and mucus. I felt my knees buckle; and as I grabbed hold of the basin I thought, 'My brain is falling apart.' The yuppy with the ponytail washing his hands in the basin next to me saw what had happened. However, rather than try to help, he bolted. I'm not sure if he screamed as he flew out the door. I tried to remain calm as my mind raced with ideas of what it could possibly be: a bit of ligament? Cartilage? Brain matter? Goodness knows I couldn't afford to lose any of that gear. After a few seconds I decided to pull on it and felt no pain. When I completely removed it, I discovered to my relief that the specialist had left four inches of gauze inside my nostril and my body was rejecting it!

There was one time when I had to self-operate on an abscess with a sharp razor. It was 7pm on the evening of my first fight in the 2000 Nationals at Brisbane — the first step towards Olympic selection. The abscess made it impossible for me to lift my left arm above my head. I was scheduled to fight at 9.30 so I was desperate. It would've been all but impossible for me to punch my way through to the second round of the tournament with my injured wing. I didn't let team management or medical staff know about my ailment because I feared they'd ban me from competing. I took a deep breath as I prepared to lance the abscess that four days earlier I had dismissed as a pimple. It grew to the size of a 10-cent piece and finally blew out to half the size of a golf ball. It became so painful I couldn't shadow box in the gym, let alone hit the pads. When I skipped, waves of pain shot through my upper torso but I gritted my teeth and soldiered on. I'm sure some people who watched me at training might've thought I was an arrogant so'n'so because I boxed a few sessions with my left arm dangling down by my side. They might've thought I was giving the impression I could win the crown with one hand.

On the day of my first fight my arm was red raw; my collarbone and left pectoral muscle were badly infected and I was worried it would be extremely hard to compete. I still have no idea why I was affected by abscesses when other boxers have never suffered them. I had one treated by the doctor before I jetted out with the Aussie team to compete for the Liverpool Cup in England. He explained an abscess is a collection of pus that is caused by an infection and it gets stored in a cavity in the muscle. It's apparently a defensive mechanism to prevent the infection from spreading to other parts of the body — tell you what, though, they kill! I knew how to remove it because I watched as the doctor cut it out from my calf. The procedure left a hole in my leg the size of a golf ball and whilst it will sound gross I was fascinated because rather than have pus ooze out like lava from a volcano, he removed a sack full of gunk. When I looked *into* the hole I was transfixed; I could see the muscle and the sheath that surrounded it. I then watched as the doctor submerged wads of cotton gauze into a dish full of antiseptic and he then stuffed them into the hole. The doctor then placed plaster over it and bandaged me up. Because I had to treat it in England the doctor showed me what I had to do — wash my hands, put gloves on, remove the bandage, tear the bandage off, rip the gauze out of the hole, squeeze saline into it, disinfect some fresh gauze and stuff it back in. Simple. I followed his orders for six days and there were no problems.

Playing Dr Dan in England paid off that evening because I gritted my teeth, raised the razor blade and sliced the infected area under my arm. I squeezed my bicep and watched with a strange fascination as this thick green and black coloured gloop oozed out of me. With each contraction of my bicep I milked the poison from my system. After 15 minutes I figured it was all gone so I jumped under a steaming hot shower and lathered the infected area with soap. With the poison removed, I went out and won a very hard fought four rounder. I was ecstatic because I had taken my first step towards making the team for the Sydney Olympics.

The last time I dealt with an abscess was at the end of a pre-Olympic tournament in Bali where one popped out of my right thigh. I'd fought a tremendous toe-to-toe battle with highly rated Italian Giacobbe Fragomeni and I learnt a lot from that bout. I ignored the pain for two days but it became too much so I again dragged out the razor. I called for my roomie, James Swan to take a look as I bit down on a towel and slowly sliced my thigh open. His turned away and fought the urge to vomit. I wouldn't recommend anyone start treating themselves for such ailments, but there was no way I was going to try my luck — or health — in the Bali hospital. While I had a badly broken nose treated in the storage room of a hospital on a remote island in the Philippines I'd heard far too many horror stories about the Bali casualty ward to allow someone to poke and prod me there.

CHAPTER 16

THE WORLD CHAMPION FLATMATE

When I moved to Sydney in 2001 to pursue my dream to become world champion my then assistant trainer Billy Hussein took me to an apartment in Bankstown in the city's sprawling south-west and introduced me to my new flatmate, Vakhtang Darchinyan, a flyweight who was reputed to boast a power-packed punch. 'Vic' was waiting in the driveway when Billy and I arrived and my first impression was of a ball of muscle with an accent like Boris Badanov in the old *Rocky and Bullwinkle* cartoon. Vic firmly shook my hand and then loudly declared, 'I … TAKE … BAGS!' Seeing as though it sounded more like an order than a friendly suggestion I didn't dare to protest. Instead I watched in amazement as Vic, who probably weighed all of 50 kilos, grabbed my luggage roughly by the handles and bounded up unbothered by what I found to be a near back-breaking weight.

I was soon sitting at the kitchen table opposite a bloke I didn't know from a bar of soap and vice versa. All I knew of

Vic was he'd represented Armenia with distinction at the 2000 Olympics by making the quarter finals (good judges say he was robbed of a medal) and Jeff Fenech had convinced him stay behind after it was over. Jeff's pitch was to follow Kostya Tszyu's lead and 'have a go' Down Under.

The clock seemed to tick loudly as we sat quietly at the table and in what I can only imagine was an attempt to break the ice, my new mate said, fondly: 'I COOK STEAK, YOU EAT.' So I watched Vic slap a slab of meat and some frozen chips in the frying pan and he seasoned it with a variety of spices I'd never heard of, let alone smelled before. I noted the look of intensity on Vic's face as he cooked the meal; he was very much a man on a mission because he focused his entire concentration on the pan. Once it was cooked — well done, if I recall correctly — he placed it proudly on a plate and then put it down in front of me with the instruction: 'EAT! YOU EAT!' With that Vic sat down, folded his arms and watched as I ate each and every mouthful. His eyes followed the choreography of the fork digging into the meat, the knife sawing into it and the meat being placed into my mouth. 'Mmmmmmm,' I said to emphasize how good it tasted. 'Thanks mate, this is great tucker.' The truth is, I wasn't really all that hungry but there was no way I was going to refuse Vic's offer. I remember seeing the stern look in his eyes and thinking, *'He's going to cook me if I don't eat this meal!'* Vic's offer to cook for me was really just an extension of the hand of friendship he'd already offered me when we met in the driveway of the apartment block.

I felt quite relaxed in Vic's company, despite our cultural differences. He was the same as me: a bloke chasing his dream to become the champion of the world and someone who wanted to secure his future. We didn't need long to become close mates because we trained hard together and supported each other as much as we could during our first couple of pro fights. In between training and fighting, we whiled away many hours playing card games. We didn't play for cash, because neither of us could afford to lose it, but the games were still very competitive.

After a month in Bankstown we went our separate ways. Nina joined me in Sydney and we set up house in a one-bedroom flat at Ashfield; Vic met Olga, a beautiful Russian lady, in the forecourt of the Sydney Opera House. Our friendship remains strong and I have watched on with pride as Vic, known internationally as the 'Raging Bull', has established himself as one of boxing's great pound-for-pound champions. It frustrates me to think that while the likes of Mike Tyson and Lennox Lewis are two massive Darchinyan fans he is still to receive the recognition he deserves from the Australian sporting public. Some people contend the reason he's still to be embraced is the language barrier, but if true that's not fair. As a fighter — and as an Australian — he should be judged solely by how he performs in the ring under the Aussie flag and, believe me, my mate gives his heart and soul. He has also worked overtime to fit in to his adopted nation, employing a voice coach to help soften his accent and he certainly loves Australia. He appreciates the values of his adopted nation and has embraced life here with passion. He is an Australian by choice and I consider him a dinky di. In many regards, Vic is the new Kostya Tszyu and in time —

hopefully, that's sooner rather than later — I'm certain he will be acknowledged as one of this nation's true sporting champions; a people's champion. He won the IBF flyweight title in Miami 2004 and is regarded as the hardest punching flyweight in the world.

Incredibly, while he can walk around Sydney largely unknown, in Armenia he is a deadset superstar. In 2006, he was showered with gifts and offerings when he visited the presidential palace; every year for the last six years Vic has been named among the president's top ten Armenians and he is a hero to millions of people. While the steak and chips the Raging Bull cooked for me was a bizarre way to start a friendship, it worked. The ties that bind Vic and I are strong, and I'm definitely the richer for it. Vic Darchinyan: tough exterior, heart of gold.

CHAPTER 17

THE TEAM

If Bankstown Police Boys Club proved one thing it was that you don't need a flash gym to produce fighters. The club was home to Team Fenech when I moved to Sydney and I remember the boxing room had grimy walls and a rough, old dirty floor. If a fighter's mouthguard hit the ground he bought a new one rather than chance putting it back in his gob. In saying that, it was the heart and soul of Australian boxing and to this day I've never been as happy in a gym as I was at Bankstown.

I'd get excited about turning up to train there. It was the domain of hungry fighters and we believed if we worked hard our dreams could come true. I enjoyed the company of the special group of people who trained there with me. Team Fenech was a veritable United Nations, with indigenous Aussies and people whose family origins stretched to Lebanon, Tunisia, Turkey, Greece, Malta, Africa, the Pacific Islands, Armenia, Russia, Thailand, the Philippines and places in between. With the Queensland cane cutter Ian

McLeod, I was the token 'Skip' — as in Skippy, a white Aussie — though it is worth mentioning that no one appeared bothered by such trivialities as race or personal beliefs. Like me, they respected a bloke for the man he was.

I developed firm friendships but just as importantly I also learned plenty about the art of fighting from blokes born with tough hides and good hearts.

One fighter I admired was Nader Hamden. He trained like a demon and we sparred a countless amount of willing rounds in the old ring that dominated the room. Boxing is a unique sport. We punched shades out of each other in that gym, but there was never any ill feeling if the other guy got one up on you. Once training was over, it was handshakes, backslaps and taking the piss out of each other. When I moved to Sydney, Nader was an established professional fighter and I considered myself fortunate to be training alongside the fighter dubbed 'Lionheart'. When I had a bad day at the office I'd get frustrated when things didn't go to plan. Nader would wait at the bottom of the steps and explain the things that were driving me crazy were all part and parcel of boxing. He said the sooner I accepted that, the sooner life would become easier — and he was right.

Two other team club members I admired were the Hussein brothers, Nedal and Hussy. Nedal — who is best known by his nickname of 'Skinny' — has no inner panic button and I quickly realised nothing seemed to upset him. But he abandoned the laidback persona the instant he climbed through the ropes. He'd drive his opponents wild by riding their punches and unloading bomb after bomb. I absorbed all

I could whenever I watched Skinny and the one thing that always impressed me was his left rip to the body; it left the likes of me on the outside of the ring breathless but it would almost destroy his opponent's rib cage. I always loved watching Skinny spar or fight; he had a great style. As for Hussy, I was well aware he was a 1996 Olympian and I considered him a legend long before I started training at Bankstown. However, he floored me at our first meeting with his warm handshake and humility. A courageous fighter, Hussy's 2005 WBC flyweight world title eliminator against the rugged Mexican Jorge Arce at Las Vegas was one of the gutsiest efforts I have witnessed. For 10 bloody rounds he and Arce fought like wolves. The Mexican won the scheduled 12 rounder, but Hussein did Australia — and himself — proud. I have watched that fight on DVD six or seven times and I admire the courage he showed under fire.

One of the quiet achievers in the gym was the third Hussein; middle brother Billy. The former amateur boxer was Jeff's assistant and more often than not the right-hand man who ran the place when Jeff was away. Billy, like his brothers, is blessed with a beautiful nature and it won me over. I openly tell people he had a positive impact on my career. Billy spent time under such trainers as Johnny Lewis and Jeff, and he was smart enough to adopt from them ideas that complemented his own unique style and it has helped him become a champion trainer. He really cares for his fighters and I was very lucky to have learnt so much from him.

We had a lot of laughs in that gym. Some really colourful characters would frequent the joint, keeping us all amused and on our toes. Jeff was usually the court jester and I developed strong stomach muscles from laughing all the bloody time. Then when it was time to work we all switched on, and the fun and games were put on the back burner.

One bloke who was a genuine inspiration was an opponent from my amateur days, Peter Manesis. I watched him evolve from a self-confessed, 133-kg, overeating, loose cannon to a contender for the Australian light-heavyweight championship in 2002. Peter shed a whopping 54kg to challenge Jason DeLisle for the national crown. It was a tremendous show of restraint and determination because at his 'peak' Peter estimated he was consuming 15,000 calories a day. Religion, allied with a trip to his parents' birthplace of Greece, turned his life around and I was pleased to see the man it made him. While Jason defeated Peter in that Australian title fight I sometimes drew strength when I was doing it tough dieting before a bout by thinking of what my old Team Fenech mate endured to not only shed that bulk but also to keep it off.

Other fighters in the gym included the Kelly brothers, Glen and Kevin, Vic Darchinyan and Shannan Taylor who were all world-title contenders. One team member I formed a close bond with was David Birchell, who as an amateur was part of Australia's President's Cup-winning team in Indonesia in 1995. Dave was an ultra classy southpaw, with skill and finesse to burn. Unfortunately the high hopes the likes of Manny Hinton (who trained former WBC light-heavyweight world champion Jeff Harding) held for Birchy were dashed when he was left fighting for his life after being hit by a car while riding to work on a bike. He recovered to fight four professional bouts for as many wins, but the effects of the accident forced him to stow his gloves away. What struck me about Dave was his integrity and the interest he showed in all the fighters. Nothing ever seemed to be a problem. I could also tell he was well schooled in the sport so I paid close attention when he spoke. Birchy played a large part in my success in winning the world title in Montreal. Jeff was away a lot and Dave oversaw a large part of my preparation.

When I split from Jeff I approached Birchy to be in my corner. He has proven over the years to be a true friend, though the traits that have endeared him to me come straight from his father, Ray. I met Ray at the 1997 Arafura Games in the Northern Territory where he gloved up the fighters before their bouts. He struck me as a nice bloke and we got on like a house on fire. Ray invited me to stay at his family home in Sydney and I was soon staying there for a week at a time during my trips to benefit from the calibre of sparring that didn't exist in Perth. Apart from providing me with my own room, Ray lent me a car and all but gave me the keys to the city. I'll never forget the kindness he and his family showed me when I was just a young amateur big on dreams and not much else, and I've tried to replicate it to up and comers as I've enjoyed some success.

There were others in the background at Bankstown who added to the atmosphere of the place, including Jeff's special mate, Con Spyrpolous. Despite his own problems in life — he was brain damaged at birth, Con brought a smile to all our faces by making it clear he loved the attention he was shown —

and that attention could have come from his trying to whack blokes with a broom. Con was flipping hilarious and was very much one of the boys. Another welcome team member was Jeff's son, Beau, a beautifully mannered kid who is rightly a source of great pride to his father. There was also Franky Gatt who helped out by taking us on the pads all the time. Franky was a likeable fella who loved the sport and the fighters. Max Simrani was always on hand to massage the boys.

One guy who deserves his own chapter in my book is Angelo Hyder. A man with zero shame, he will do anything, anywhere, anytime for a laugh. A crowd pleaser, he has a unique way of making people crack up, even when the joke is on them. His humour isn't intended to demean or belittle people, the opposite really. He just loves making people laugh, either with him or at him. 'H' has been my matchmaker since day one and has also been a very important component of my corner, reading the fights and my opponent very well. A staunch family man, I'm sure his household is never dull or quiet. He has a very sharp mind and thinks outside the box, though some of his ideas are way out there. A boxer in the army, Angelo is also an experienced trainer, though I tend to tape his mouth shut when training starts because he loves a chat. Angelo has manoeuvred not only myself, but just about every other Aussie boxer in the past eight years into title shots or big fights. He has all the international contacts and when it comes to the crunch his laconic manner seals the deal. Not only does H know the fight game very well and he reads a fight sharply, he's always thinking of ways to help a fighter improve. He was great to have in the corner because he remained cool in a crisis and I found I fed off his positive energy. If ever I need a laugh I punch his number into my phone and when I hear his trademark answer of 'R-r-r-r-ighto', it's on, jokes and laughs.

The Bankstown Police Boys Club boxing room — we all walked through its old doors hungry fighters and left better people for the friendships and the experiences we shared there. It was a magic place and any gym that can replicate the feeling of brotherhood we enjoyed in Team Fenech's early days, I guarantee you one thing — it'll produce great fighters.

CHAPTER 18

SHOWDOWN IN BANKSTOWN

My mum, who is used to the laidback lifestyle of Perth, wondered what on earth she had walked into when I made my professional debut on 29 June 2001 at the Bellevue Function Centre in Bankstown. There was nothing wrong with the place; it was actually quite nice but what shocked Mum — and the rest of my clan for that matter — was when the security guards honed in on her and used a metal detector to ensure she wasn't trying to smuggle a weapon into the fight. Luckily, Mum wasn't packing an AK-47 or any grenades on that particular night so she entered the premises without causing a scene.

My professional debut was against a Fijian named Waqa Kolivuso.

I didn't know too much about the bloke except he was about to fight his third professional bout after being knocked out in his previous two by Rasheed Kadoebi (the first Pakistan-born fighter to ever win a professional title when he beat Joel Burke for the NSW belt in Dubbo) and Sakio Bika, who was a member of Cameroon's Olympic team that fought at Sydney and later on in life challenged Joe Calzaghe and Markus Beyer for their world titles. He also won the 'Contender' title, Sylvester Stallone's reality television boxing show. Sakio and I sparred countless rounds together, and when people ask me what he is like as a fighter, my response is standard as it is honest: He would give King Kong a hard fight! Ours was the first fight on the card. The adrenaline surged through my veins because I wasn't fighting for a trophy this time, I was fighting for my livelihood.

To have Jeff Fenech behind me as my trainer made me feel invincible. I listened to Jeff and Billy when they said not to rush the fight and risk making a mistake that could leave me vulnerable. I followed their advice and spent the opening round 'sussing' out my opponent to find any weaknesses that could be exploited. There were plenty, and by the second round it was obvious our fight was a mismatch as I put Waqa away quickly. I hit him with a jab to the body, went upstairs, threw another jab and then unleashed a hook to the top of his head. His reaction to the hook was to put his hands up high so I landed a good right to his body and the hands came down. I landed a solid right on his jaw and he went down like a sack of spuds.

While it wasn't an especially hard fight I was elated — and I admit, relieved — to have won. I did the job with crisp, clean punches and was satisfied. It didn't feel anything like my victory over the Brazilian at the Sydney Olympics where my head almost exploded with excitement and a sense of achievement but I was, however, thankful I'd started the most important stage of my career in the best way possible.

My joy was somewhat tempered, though, 40 minutes after the fight when I saw my beaten opponent sitting alone in the back of the hall. I felt no remorse whatsoever knocking him out but he was a bloody long way from home and the people who cared for him. I couldn't help but feel for him so I arranged for the centre's manager to give him a decent feed and a soft drink. Judging by the way Waqa proceeded to wolf down his feed the poor bloke was starving. When he finished we shook hands and I wished him well. His career was short-lived. In his next bout he was knocked out by Steve McIvor in the first round and he decided to retire.

CHAPTER 19

DANIEL IN THE LIONS' DEN

The boxing ring is no place for the faint hearted but I will say that nothing matches the gut-churning terror of being locked in a cage with six extremely agitated lions. I know this because in 2002 I made the mistake of entering a lions' den and allowing the door to be locked behind me. While I have a namesake mentioned in the Holy Bible for winning favour with a lion when he wrenched a thorn from one of its mighty paws, I made no pals among this particular pride of man-eaters. Instead I left a couple of them nursing massive headaches when I was forced to unleash two punches that would've knocked any of my opponents cold.

Not long after I moved to Sydney to fight under Jeff Fenech I drove past a circus that had set up camp at a reserve just outside Bankstown. By no stretch of the imagination was it Cirque du Soleil. But it had clowns and acrobats, a big top, a few rides, coloured lights and dodgy carnival tucker. The jewel in this particular circus's crown was the lions' cage that was home to three females and three males, including a moth-eaten bastard whose face was not only criss-crossed with deep scars but had a look that suggested he was permanently pissed off with the world. Considering the life he led he probably had good reason to be ticked off. He was cooped up in a cage for most of the day and forced to do mind-numbing tricks over and over again for kids and their grandparents. His birthright was to reign as king of the jungle, but fate had been cruel and condemned him to being the star attraction of a travelling circus. His female companions appeared equally put out.

The first time the king of the cage laid eyes on me he dismissed me with a lazy yawn. The second time he saw me I had trespassed upon his territory and belted members of his harem with powerful right hands. Yep, he showed a much greater interest in my presence then by making threatening gestures that scared the crap out of me.

When Nina and I visited the circus I had just started to get a profile in the Sydney media courtesy of a couple of quick knockout victories. The two young blokes whose job was to take care of the big cats were boxing nuts and they recognised me. We spoke for a few minutes and they invited me to join them inside the cage. Nina couldn't believe that I agreed but it seemed like a great idea at the time. However, within a few seconds of entering the cage and hearing the door shut I realised my error of judgement. My escorts had disappeared to clean and feed the big cats when one of the lionesses decided to introduce herself to me by repeatedly butting her head into my midriff — and it hurt.

'Just belt her, Danny,' yelled one of the handlers in between shovelling a mound of lion's crap into a bucket. 'Give her a good crack on the chops to let her know who's boss.'

It felt wrong to hurt the creature but she butted me again in the gut with a blow that was much harder than the others.

'Dan,' yelled the second handler. 'You have to hit her or else she'll be all over you.'

With that I clenched my fist, recoiled it to my shoulder as if it was a tight spring and let go but the blow I delivered wouldn't have bruised a grape. There was no commitment to the punch because I just couldn't bring myself to hit the animal even though I was absolutely shitting myself.

'Mate, hit her harder,' screamed the first bloke. 'She will go you.'

The lioness used his command as the signal to unleash a body blow that pushed me back a step or two. With that I locked and loaded my right hand and landed a beauty on the side of her snout. I waited a scary split second for a meaty paw to claw my skin in retaliation, but it didn't come. She instead nuzzled up against my leg like a pleasant domestic cat.

'Nice punch, Danny. Now give it to the one behind you,' yelled the other lad, who clearly was enjoying the exhibition.

I unleashed another 'lion tamer' and she, too, became immediately submissive. Rather than feel like a gladiator in a coliseum in Ancient Rome I felt more like a prized goose. Not only had I allowed myself to get locked in a cage but I was punching on with a pride of lions. The boss of the cage was ropable. He displayed enough signs for me to realise I'd outstayed my welcome. I wanted out. I almost pooped my pants when I realised the lion with the deep scars on his face and his two bodyguards weren't locked in a separate cage. The big bloke pushed the iron gate open, romped down the ramp towards me and then bunted me fair in the guts. The hairs on the back of my neck stood up and a cold sweat formed above my brow.

'Boys,' I said, the urgency obvious in my voice. 'I ... want ... out ... right ... now!'

The dynamic duo sprung straight into action like Batman and Robin. As they distracted the lions I was advised not to run to the gate.

'Stay calm, Danny,' said one as he waved a rag in front of the angry male lion. 'If you run he'll go for you.'

I am not ashamed to admit it took all my nerve not to break into a blind-panicked sprint for the door. A boxing ring or a lion's cage? Lead me to the ring any day.

CHAPTER 20

SUFFERING FOR THE ART

It doesn't matter if you're a world champion or a preliminary fighter, the time that is needed to train, rest, recover and treat injuries in-between bouts makes professional boxing a fulltime job. There can be no half measures. As a sport it's too dangerous an occupation to give anything less than total commitment. That can mean getting up before sunrise in the middle of winter for roadwork; it can mean staying up all night with your hand in a bucket of ice to reduce swelling; it can mean starving yourself to make weight; it can mean refraining from sex for weeks at a time because some blokes say it keeps their legs strong; it can mean a bad day at the office is to finish sparring sessions with a broken vertebrae in your back; it can mean facing the disappointment of defeat. Once you step through those ropes you are on your own, unlike football there's no team-mate there to take a hit while you catch your breath. There is an old saying that the light of day will illuminate what was done in the dark of night, yet it never ceases to amaze me to see on just about every card be it at the ritzy MGM Casino at Las Vegas or a humble RSL club west of the Black Stump there'll always be a fighter who hasn't put the hours in — and it shows when he's used as a punching bag by his opponent. As they get belted from pillar to post I can't help but ask myself, 'Mate, why do this to yourself?' I don't judge them because we all fight for different reasons. Perhaps they were called up at the last minute or maybe they need to find cash to pay some outstanding bills. However, I will say to go into the ring underdone is as senseless as it is dangerous. From a professional viewpoint it's not only unfair on the fighter's trainer, the promoter and the people who pay good money to see an evenly matched contest, it's grossly unfair to the boxer himself. Could you imagine a surgeon who skipped a few lectures at university fronting up to do a delicate operation? When a fighter puts his gloves on he's up against many things. The last thing he should be fighting is himself.

My belief was always if I expected to be called 'professional' I need to act that way in the gym, during road runs, at the meal table and in the public arena. However, I know only too well it isn't easy for any fighter in the early stage of his career to follow the lifestyle of an Oscar De La Hoya or Kostya Tszyu because Kostya and Oscar are only in their position after years of doing the hard yards.

For 99 per cent of fighters life is a constant juggling act to train, (in some cases) to look after their family and to hold down a job that pays the rent and puts food on the table. In the early stages of any professional fighter's career the money they make from fighting is no more than a few thousand dollars at a time — if they're lucky. The bigger purses come as they establish a record and reputation but that takes time and it takes sacrifice. There is plenty of stress involved in making ends meet financially and, just as importantly, emotionally. Very few people outside the game can understand the stress a fighter experiences as he rushes from his home to the gym to the workplace back to the gym and home again. Believe me, it's not fun — I've known of guys to arrive to the gym with tears of frustration in their eyes because their load eventually crushes them — and that isn't good for their blood pressure least of all their mental health.

I was lucky. When I moved to Sydney, Nina accepted I was on a mission to become world champion. I'm not saying it was easy for her but Nina appreciated that this meant almost everything would be focused towards us achieving that goal. She shared the dream, and her love and support helped me big time, even when we spent our first four months in a one-bedroom shoebox that backed on to what I reckon is the busiest railway line in the world. She understood I needed to train, watch tapes of my opponents, spend hours with Jeff and the boys from the gym, go to sleep early and that I needed to follow a strict diet. She also understood the possibility of mood swings because the nature of boxing is one day you're up as everything looks great, but the following day you can turn into a bastard because of a hand injury or a fight falling through. Sometimes I think a boxer's partner needs to be stronger than the fighter.

I was also lucky with sponsorship. Most businesses don't want to be associated with the fight game because over the years the sport has regrettably gained, a grubby reputation for double dealing, petty politics, backstabbing and character assassination. But not too long after I settled in Sydney two champion blokes named Henk and Arie Plug from Leichhardt Electrical Wholesalers took a punt and backed me.

The pair's generosity was humbling. When they heard Nina and I were setting up our home in Ashfield they gave us a second-hand fridge and a washing machine to save us from having to buy whitegoods. They invited us to their homes on so many occasions I wouldn't even try to put a number on the meals we shared while neither of them have ever failed to make us feel welcome. No matter where in the world I fought they were there in their Green Machine T-shirts. I'll never be able to repay them for their contribution to my fight career.

In the early stages of my professional career I'd be out running on my own around Ashfield Park at 9 or 10 o'clock at night and I'd hammer myself. I'd do at least an hour's worth of short sprints and a series of 400-metre runs and while I did that because I was hungry to succeed, I also wanted to gain a psychological boost over my future opponents. You see, as I worked up a sweat I'd imagine them rugged up in bed or stretched out on their couch drinking a cup of hot coffee while they watched television. Those mental images made me feel quite happy because I figured my extra work would give me a massive advantage over them if beating them came down to a matter of fitness or a battle of wills. I was also racing the clock because when I turned professional I was 27, so that made me an 'old' rookie. I appreciated very early in the piece that I didn't have time to stuff around. I realised if I was going to get anywhere in boxing I needed to get there quickly so I embraced sacrifice and discipline as the cornerstones of my new career.

CHAPTER 21

HUNGER

Before a fight a boxer must conquer his toughest opponent — his mind. Some people call the mental obstacles we have to overcome demons but I call them sacrifices. In my case the sacrifices were: being separated from my family when I left Perth six weeks out from a bout to train at my base in Sydney; mood swings that struck like a sucker punch at any stage of the preparation; the ritual called dieting; and the physical pain I endured at training. I never had the mortgage on sacrifice and self-deprivation; they are the lot of all serious fighters.

I'm confident any non-heavyweight boxer from any era would agree with me when I say that apart from climbing through the ropes to fight, the toughest part of boxing is making weight. The scales monitor a boxer's discipline and his will power. The dread of *failing* is always with you: the weigh-in is the fighter's deadline. If he hasn't been honest and comes in too heavy it could mean the fight will be called off, and for me *that* would have been too much to take because it'd mean those weeks of training, formulating strategies and living in isolation from the real world would count for nothing. If the fight was deemed a 'catch weight' because one opponent is heavier than the other, the bout can't be classed as a title fight. Again, a wasted opportunity.

With that worry constantly on my mind the pressure not to indulge at the meal table was always present, so I went to bed hungry. When people talk about a prizefighter's hunger they're talking about a desire that comes from chasing a dream with next to nothing in your stomach. Sometimes I started to diet four months out from a bout, and while that might sound like a snack to some people, remember this: my working day consisted of two intense running sessions starting at 7am, punching pads, working out on the heavy bag and speed ball, sparring and pumping weights. The result was I burnt a massive number of calories. By dinner time I was famished. But I could never eat as much as I wanted. If there was no restriction on me I'd have eaten about three times as much as the portions I allowed myself. A lot of the time you craved fluid, but even that has to be closely monitored. I can push my body through exhaustion; I endured all sorts of physical pain — and even ask for more — but those hunger pangs were something else. The grind of boxing has allowed me to sympathise with people who are denied food because of the country they're born in or life's circumstances. In the countdown to a bout there was no escape from that pit in my stomach. If I turned on the television I did so knowing there was bound to be a commercial promoting the latest taste sensation and that was only going to make me want to eat. If I opened a magazine I did so at the risk of seeing glossy photos of gourmet meals. When I walked down cosmopolitan King Street in Sydney's Newtown I knew I'd be bombarded by an assortment of aromas that wafted out from exotic restaurants. Even though my mouth salivated on those occasions at the thought of sitting down and eating to my heart's content I *needed* to remain strong and keep my mouth closed.

My normal weight was 85kg and my waist is 82cm — that's a boy's size. However to fight a light-heavyweight I had to hit the scales at no more than 79.4kg. I needed to drop 6kg, and while it was tough it was nowhere near as hard as the days when I fought as a super-middleweight. That weight limit is 76.2kg and while I won that world title, it almost killed me making weight. While some people rate giving up grog a sacrifice, I abstained from drinking alcohol for the good of my performance in the ring for long stretches since 1997. What I missed wasn't the mere act of drinking a beer, it was the fun my mates and I had on a night out. We're pretty loose and we do push the envelope and so some crazy things, but they're done at our own expense. We don't impose our idea of fun on strangers or passersby. I don't live the life a lot of people might expect of a champion boxer. I don't go to flash nightclubs; I don't expect my name to be included on VIP lists; I don't expect free drinks, I'm happy to pay; I'm happy to meet people who support me but I don't go much for backslaps and false praise. There are some fighters who embrace that lifestyle but I get more out of the idea that one day I'll be picking up my kids from school or coaching their sporting teams. I think there comes a time when everyone looks back on their life and I'm already certain that when that day comes for me I'll be happy to think I paid for those drinks and I didn't surround myself with fair-weather friends.

I missed Perth when I prepared for a bout. Obviously what I missed most was Nina, Chloe, Archie, my family and friends. The silence of the big house at Newtown got to me most of all. I missed the noise of Chloe's size-one shoes galloping up the hallway. I didn't have Chloe climbing all over me, hanging off my neck or ripping at my hair. I missed that like crazy when I transplanted myself to the harbour city to try and focus on fighting. Nina has obviously had to shoulder plenty of sacrifice along the way, too, because I know she was lonely when I was not around for weeks at a time. I'd think of that when I trained because it would've be an insult to her not to give a session everything I had when I was away from her. I'd phone home all the time, but it wasn't the same as being there. When Nina and I decided I'd give professional boxing a go we had no idea of how it would pan out. Thankfully it was successful and now it is over we agree the sacrifices have been worthwhile.

I reminded myself during the tough times that I was putting myself through what I did to set our family up for a secure future. When you set yourself a goal you don't just go for it when you feel good and refreshed and when the weather is fine. It is a 24 hour a day, seven days a week, 52 week a year commitment. You follow that dream when it would be so easy to give up, when it would be so easy just to turn your back on it. I achieved my goal.

I've said it before but a fighter endures massive mood swings before a bout. One day you might have a sensational session but the next get some news from home or a friend that flattens your spirit and makes life appear grim. A lot of negativity can cross a fighter's mind when he thinks about a bout and it can be very, very heavy. I tried to keep the mood as bright and light as possible. It could be a battle to maintain that state of mind. I knew what I was in life: a professional boxer. And I appreciated that it was one of the toughest professions in the world. I loved what I did and I treated the hardships as steps towards my ultimate goal of being the light-heavyweight champion of the world.

CHAPTER 22

OPPORTUNITY RINGS

Had I known the news I was about to hear when the phone rang one evening, I would've dived over the lounge, commando rolled through the doorway and into the hall to grab it. Jeff Fenech was on the other end and he was absolutely *buzzing*.

'Greeny,' he yelled. 'They're giving us a shot at Beyer! What do you think?'

What did I think? It was my dream come true. It was my opportunity to set Nina, Chloe and me up for life. It was the moment I'd been sweating on for as long as I could remember, so I gave a thoughtful response: Let's flog him.'

However as is often the case with boxing, there was a but … the promoters who looked after the German WBC super-middleweight champion Markus Beyer were prepared to pay me only $US30,000. It was a hell of a lot less than what most people would probably expect a world-title contender to receive, because when people talk about big fights they normally think of million-dollar pay days. The purse Beyer's people offered didn't change my approach in the slightest. If anything, I considered the money a bonus because I would've fought for free.

When I returned to the lounge room Nina simply nodded when I told her it was Jeff and, oblivious to the fireworks going off in my head, she went back to watching the TV. After two minutes I cleared my throat and said: 'Hey, Bub, we got the world title shot!' It was like Christmas. We hugged and started laughing insanely. The title shot was as much a reward for her love, support, honesty and loyalty as it was for my training and fighting. Even though Chloe was only one-and-a-half at the time we woke her to join in the celebration. She had no idea what was going on, but as my most cherished treasure I wanted her to share the moment. I phoned my dad first.

I did my research and discovered Beyer was a two-time Olympian, had enjoyed 27 victories from 28 fights and was very balanced and skilful. He would easily be the best of the 16 fighters I'd faced — and knocked out. However my view was that he had two hands and a head and it would be up to me to hit him. I understood that no one had ever put pressure on him, and that was my plan. Indeed, Jeff reinforced my view to go for broke by saying I'd need to take risks because I wouldn't win Beyer's crown by simply tapping away.

It isn't all that well known but after my fifteenth professional bout I was offered the opportunity to fight Germany's other world champion (IBF and WBA) super-middleweight, Sven Ottke. He was known to Australian fight fans because he iced Anthony Mundine with a knockout punch in the tenth round of their IBF title bout in 2001. Under the terms offered by the Germans I had four weeks to get ready for it, and while I was tempted to fight I decided to let my head — and not my heart — rule on that occasion. I had always promised myself that I wouldn't just fight for a world title but I would win the belt. While I realised it would be a huge honour to be in a position where you were considered worthy enough to contest the world championship, I wanted more than that. I wanted to go all the way. I was contracted to fight Jason DeLisle and I thought I needed a solid victory against an opponent of his calibre before I fought for the world title. I also had another reason for rejecting the Ottke opportunity. You see, he enjoyed a home-town advantage every time he entered the ring because all but one of his fights had been held in Germany (his sole 'foreign' bout was held in neighbouring Austria). I'd heard rumblings that he had benefited from some questionable decisions on more than one occasion. The more people I spoke to the more I heard Germany was a place to avoid fighting in at all costs because if their boxer didn't get you, the judges or other ringside officials would. That feedback did little to make me want to fly to Europe. Had Ottke been willing to fight me on neutral territory I would have jumped at the chance. While I knew it was the best decision for my career I don't mind admitting I wondered how long it'd take before I received a second shot.

While Ottke defeated Englishman David Starie over 12 rounds, I demolished DeLisle in five solid rounds. Apart from the confidence I gained from such an emphatic victory over Jason I also gained a top 10 ranking in the WBC. My entry into the top 10 prompted Ottke's management, who also looked after Beyer, to offer me a shot at the latter. They seemed very keen to get me over to Germany and I can only imagine that was because they considered me to be little or no threat to either of their men. It was up to me to change that perception.

The day after Jeff's call I skipped into training and it was hard to contain my excitement. I sparred sharply and was so lucky to have the world-class Paul Miller to train with because, like Beyer, 'Mr Magic' was a southpaw. While he lacked the experience of the world champion, he was technically just as sound. I had a tremendous preparation for the fight. I was up before sunrise doing sit-ups and running the steep man-made hills in the Olympic precinct at Homebush. Every punch I threw at training had purpose. My entire life was focused on bringing the belt back to Australia. However, the veteran fight commentator Colonel Bob Sheridan said I'd need to fight more than Beyer. He said the German scene was a disgrace and cited his experience when the South African Francois 'the White Rhino' Botha beat Axel Shultz in their IBF heavyweight fight in 1995 (Botha failed a drug test and was stripped of the title) and the crowd went crazy, pelting the ring with champagne bottles. If the Colonel didn't fear for his life then, he had good reason to be scared later when he and Don King and everyone else involved with the promotion needed a police escort to the airport.

'I was out of bed at 3am,' he said. 'We needed a police escort. There were 100 cops. There had been death threats to Don King, Carl King … I was only the announcer, why were they going to kill me?'

Rather than be worried by Bob's horror story, my view was that if the crowd was booing me and carrying on then that was a good sign for me; it would mean I was doing something right — beating their champion

CHAPTER 23

THE CHALLENGER

When I entered Markus 'Boom Boom' Beyer's gym to attend a public training session to promote our bout the WBC world champion jumped off a table to greet me in a way that suggested we were old friends. Beyer smiled and tried to charm me, but I took it as a front. He was playing a mind game. He was the spider trying to lure me, the fly, into his web because he wanted me to see him as a nice guy, not my opponent. But I wanted him to know where we stood from the outset. I was there to destroy him and take the title back to Australia.

I was sweltering in a European heatwave because I wanted his crown. When Beyer offered me his hand to allow the press photographers to capture the moment when the champion met his latest challenger, I latched on to it aggressively and dragged it so it rested above my heart. I wanted the champ to feel that my heartbeat was steady and strong. It was not, as he may have expected, racing out of control like a drummer in a punk band. Even though I was only days away from the biggest fight of my career he could feel that I was calm and far from overawed by the occasion. My other hand was wrapped around his neck to make it impossible for him to step away from me. I wanted him to feel trapped. Suffocated. I refused to loosen my grip even when he tried to break free. Beyer was rattled, and while small beads of sweat surfaced on his forehead he maintained his smile for the cameras. He was selling himself as the champion, while I stared, hungry and emotionless, into the cameras. I was the challenger and I wanted Beyer to know that I meant business. Beyer knew I was switched on. He could smell a battle looming and his body language suggested he did not like it.

The next time Beyer and I crossed paths was just four days before the bout. He was all business. The warm, welcoming smile was replaced by the look of a haunted man who'd realised he would need to dig deep to hang on to what was his. He did not offer his handshake as freely as at our first meeting. While he avoided eye contact, I remained carefree and happy. I lapped up the moment as Beyer and I shared centre stage at a press conference alongside some famous German racing drivers who'd burnt rubber on the Nürburgring racetrack the night before. Beyer and I were scheduled to fight in a big tarpaulin that would be set up on the track. Bernd Schneider, who drove for Mercedes, was among the drivers, and I told him how much I admired his handiwork. The press conference was very stiff, so I amused myself. I told the local media I was a tank driver in the Australian army and chuckled to myself as they scribbled that down. Fortunately none of them thought to ask me about the workings of a panzer. One said that I looked relaxed. I was. Fighting for a world title was a dream come true. I intended to savour as much of the experience as I could.

After the presser (press conference) Beyer and I were asked to put on racing driver's suits for yet another photo opportunity. When I was all kitted out I asked Schneider to take me for a spin and the look on the German promoters was pure 24 carat gold. They couldn't believe a boxer on the eve of a world title bout was prepared to drive in a car that hit speeds of 270 kilometres on hour. Yeeeehaaah! We did five laps of the circuit and the television cameramen lapped it up. Inside the car Schneider really worked the back straight. As the speedometer hit 270k's per hour I wrestled with some wicked G-forces. It was a great sensation and it allowed me to take my mind off the fight. For the life of me, I couldn't understand why Beyer didn't have a go.

The champ and I crossed paths again at the weigh-in and by that time my crew had flown in en masse from Australia to support me. The locals had no idea what hit them when Lowy, Dave, Jesa, Wizza and his cousin Clint, Brooksy, Henk, Arie, Bowdo, John Hall, Mick Pember, Locko, Molly, Cappo and Pauline joined my family. The mood among the Aussies reflected my own, playful and buoyant. Beyer looked constipated by comparison. I leapt onto the scales and was under weight thanks to the 'consideration' of my hosts. Despite their swearing blind that the scales used at the official weigh-in were accurate, the data they fed me was wrong and meant I had to diet even harder in the days before the weigh-in. I had my suspicions about the validity of the scales, but what do you do?

It was just another of their tricks, but rather than bite I let it go. Instead I surveyed the scene and let rip the rallying cry that rang out during the Sydney Olympics: 'Aussie ... Aussie ... Aussie' and the crew thundered as one: 'Oi ...Oi ... Oi.' Perhaps it was the rawness of the scene that seemed to freak Beyer out. The champion climbed onto the scales to polite applause but then, to his amazement, people started to point and laugh at him. He didn't realise at first what the joke was, but the media captured it. I was making rabbit ears behind his head as he stood flexing his muscles. When Markus realised the laugh was on him he didn't see the humour in it. I thought what the hell. Beyer was going to try and KO me the next day and I was going to try and do the same to him. I thought one of us might as well enjoy himself while we waited for our date with destiny.

D-Day and I'd slept like a kitten, largely thanks to Billy Mead who went beyond the call of duty to stand guard outside my room. We feared Beyer's crowd might try to disturb my sleep so he took it upon himself to stand to all night. The big fella ensured I wasn't disturbed. He was as vigilant as a pit bull patrolling a scrap metal yard because he even refused to allow the hotel cleaners to drag their trolleys and vacuum cleaners past his checkpoint.

Sadly, I couldn't bring myself to thank the driver who'd been assigned by the promoter to drive me to the venue. On the previous two trips with Marco it had taken no more than

45 reasonably comfortable minutes. However, for reasons I still can't fathom — and Marco, himself, couldn't explain at the time — it took one and a half hours to make the same journey on fight night, even though the traffic wasn't excessive. I had two choices as Marco feigned confusion: either to lose it or to settle back and listen to the music pumping through my headphones. I chose to chill. I wasn't going to do what the Germans wanted and lose my focus.

I'll never forget the mass of people heading towards the doors of the venue. They were *everywhere*, and because the van had my name and the date of my fight with Beyer emblazoned on it, they knew where to direct their abuse. I didn't care. I just sat back and enjoyed the show with a big grin on my face.

Common courtesy normally dictates that a world-title contender is provided with a private dressing room, but on my arrival at the racetrack I discovered the promoters had allowed some preliminary fighters to use my room. While it wasn't their fault, Steve Bowden gave them short shift, yelling, in colourful language, for them to get their bags and get out. I don't know if those blokes spoke a word of English, but 'Bowdo' didn't need to be translated. His tone said it all. The prelim fighters were wise; they took the tip and scarpered.

There was time to kill before my fight so rather than sit in the bunker, I joined the crowd and watched a few rounds of the heavyweight slugfest between Aussie Bob Mirovic and the Russian giant Nikolai Valuev (an eventual WBA champion). It was a wild and woolly battle and it helped get my heart pumping. Bob lost on points, but from what I saw 'the Big Bear' left nothing in the tank. It was a great effort and set a high benchmark for me.

A representative from Beyer's entourage watched as Jeff wrapped my hands to ensure we didn't pack a horseshoe or lump of iron in my gloves. I learnt much later that he was spooked by my calmness. He didn't see a challenger jiggling his legs or shaking in his boots. Instead I took the piss out of the boys, had a laugh and savoured the moment. When Angelo Hyder returned from Beyer's room, where he'd acted as my observer, he said it was like a morgue in there. I liked what I heard. When Jeff and I did our pad work I had just one thought as I hammered away: 'No going back ... No going back, now.'

I was ushered into a small room with my team as we waited for the television director to give us the thumbs up to make my entry. In the two minutes I waited there I turned to my brother, kissed him on the cheek and said: 'Let's do this.' I then turned to Jeff and hugged him, vowing: 'I'm gonna flog him, Jeff.' He was calm, confident and in charge and said he knew I would. I felt so proud and pumped I nearly kicked the door down in my desperation to get into the ring and to get it on. I was about to do what I had been preparing for for 12 years of my life — to fight for a world title.

CHAPTER 24

MUGGED IN GERMANY

For eleven minutes I was the WBC world super-middleweight champion and had the referee gone to the scorecard as he was heard to say on television, 'As I interpret the rules it goes to the scorecard … I can't change the rules … It's going to a decision … They're WBC's rules,' I would have walked out of the arena with the belt wrapped around my waist. But German cunning intervened. In a matter of mad seconds I had a big decision to make. *A big decision.* I was in the middle of the ring wondering how I could be denied Beyer's crown. I was looking down upon a 6000-strong crowd baying for my blood. I needed to decide whether to cave into my anger — the most blinding rage I'd ever experienced — and to start hooking every bastard in the ring or I could instead take a deep breath, remain calm and defuse what had fast become a potentially volatile situation. I have to tell you, there was a voice inside my head telling me to go wild and lash out, but a quick look ringside convinced me to remain calm. For sitting among the throng of people was my wife, my mother and my father and there was no way I would dare to put them at risk because I knew once I started throwing punches, it would spark a riot and people would get seriously hurt.

In the seconds that immediately followed my decision to relax I felt a strange calm wash over me. I am a proud fighter and I wanted to walk out of that place with my head held high. There'd be no tantrums. No tears. Beyer, head bowed, stood in the ring with the belt wrapped around him. He looked every bit like a man who'd been flogged, yet I made a point of shaking his hand even though my every instinct was to slap him *and* his team. I had lots of people at home watching me, and I like to think I had to set an example of sportsmanship and control. As I would say to the German media afterwards, I couldn't understand how he could sleep well that night knowing I had destroyed him and that I, not him, was the real world champion.

When I climbed through the ropes and made my way back towards the dressing room, the fairer members of Beyer's supporters — and I have to hand it to them, there were a few — gave me a round of applause. They knew who'd really won, and I acknowledged their honesty. In the change room, I grabbed Jeff, who looked as if he was on a mission to kick the place in, and told him to relax and to let it go. We had every right to feel as if we should go crazy; every reason to be pissed off about my being mugged in front of an international television audience. But no matter how many bones we broke or buses we overturned in our rage, it would have no bearing on the result. To this day I still don't know but, in my opinion, the rules were thrown out the window when the referee changed his original insistence to follow the rules and go for the scorecards after I flogged Beyer for five brutal rounds. I smashed him up bad but the aftermath of the ruling tarnished the world-title belt and sullied my outlook on the sport I loved.

I told BG I intended to open the fight by launching a big right hand when the ref said to come fighting so I charged towards him and — *whooshker* — Right from the outset I was on fire. I unleashed a murderous right hand but Beyer saw it coming and easily avoided it. After that I quickly turned to my corner who knew I'd planned to throw a king hit to start proceedings, and I smiled at them; such was my relaxed mental state. I followed up with a series of jabs that were as wicked as they were crisp, and found myself hitting the world champion at will. I moved forward and after one-and-a-half minutes I caught him clean on the chin with a nice right hand. He stiffened up, his eyes rolled to the back of his head and he crashed to the canvas. I was ecstatic, thinking I'd KO'd him, but the count seemed snail slow!

In the break between the first and second rounds, Beyer looked a broken man. Jeff and the boys were beaming. I hadn't even broken out into much of a sweat and halfway through the second round Beyer hit the deck again. It was all too easy. When he got back to his feet I landed a straight jab that pinned him on the ropes and then unleashed a left hook, opening up a cut over Beyer's right eye. Fighters target an opponent's cuts because if we can make them bleed badly enough the referee will stop the fight and award a TKO. You learn to 'read' the severity of cuts and I could see it was at least one-and-a-half inches long and very deep. So I tried to open it up even more. Yet the referee deducted a point for the blow that cut him when the second round finished.

By the third round I was painting the canvas red with Beyer's blood, flogging him. But the judges awarded the next round to the German!

By the fifth I'd established enough of a lead to settle back in and take control of the fight — the champion's eye was basically hanging out of his head — Beyer then butted *me* square in the face after missing with a punch. Following that exchange I felt him try to throw me down, but I was stronger than him so I resisted falling to the canvas. Beyer instead went down. The referee saw fit to warn *me* for throwing! He then turned and looked at Beyer's cut, motioning to the judges that it was caused by a butt from me! I went berserk. 'It was a fucking punch you fucking idiot!' I screamed at the ref and I screamed it to my corner and then once again at the ref. I couldn't believe what was happening. Jeff was also going off his head. But there was no other option but to suck in some air and press on. I threw a right hand that just about dropped Beyer and began smashing him with some bombs. We got entangled in a clinch; which felt like fighting an octopus. I wanted to throw a left hook at Beyer, because we were in a clinch to make some room and leverage some power, I dipped to my left and came up with a left hook. It's a rough and fairly crude move, but completely within the rules, and my objective was met when I landed the sweetest left hook to his chin. But split seconds before that, we clashed heads. Beyer winced. I could tell he was going to use the cut to find a way out of the deep hole I had thrown him in, and the referee seemed happy to oblige his pantomime.

My head went nowhere near the cut. The replay showed me brush Beyer's jaw and ear, and the ringside doctor said Beyer could not continue, which under normal circumstances meant a TKO victory in *my* favour. But instead the referee deducted one point for an intentional headbutt! I was enraged, but thought I was three points ahead on the cards. Then the ref deducted one more point for no apparent reason. The whole scene was ludicrous as it was bizarre. When it went to the scorecards, however I felt something bad was afoot. I'd been told at the pre-fight meeting that the ref would make a decision in the event of a head cut. The ref had the final decision and he was heard saying on TV, even after he deducted points, 'I don't feel it was flagrant enough that we had to disqualify the boxer …' The whole place was on edge. Billy Mead and Steve Bowden came towards the ring to offer me protection in case the joint exploded, but I yelled at them to protect my family instead. Eleven minutes I stood there waiting for the referee to make a decision. I was told to relax. Angelo Hyder had seen the scorecards and he assured me I was the champion of the world. I liked the sound of that so I asked Angelo to say it again. Yet, I felt an unpleasant sting in the pit of my stomach and with good reason, in my opinion, the ringside doctor was attempting to overrule the referee. How was that possible? And why was the doctor having any input anyway? His job was to look after the welfare of the fighters. Once he made his decision to stop the fight he should've been seen and not heard. He'd convinced the judges I'd opened a second cut on Beyer's eye with an intentional headbutt. There had only been one cut, the wound caused by a punch. It was so severe, the bout should have been stopped in the third round but the WBC officials accepted the doctor's advice as gospel. I found out later on the ring announcer was set to declare me the new world champion by TKO when he was told to wait. When he finally made his announcement he instead revealed I'd been disqualified.

CHAPTER 25

THE BITTEREST BLOW

Sunrise the morning after I'd been ripped off for the world title and I sat with nine of the boys on makeshift seats outside a BP service station drinking beer from five litre kegs BG had bought from inside the garage. While it was a far cry from the celebrations we'd hoped for, we showed typical Aussie resourcefulness to use the flat surface of the air compressor and water bay as our bar while a tinny loudspeaker attached to a pole near the petrol bowsers pumped out music. Had I not being trying to wash the dreadful taste of being disqualified out of my mouth it could have been quite a party. It took a lot of control to hold off the tears of disappointment that were welling deep within me. I maintained my fight face by urging the gang to drink up because my loss to Beyer wasn't the end of the world and that I figured we may as well enjoy the rest of our time in Germany.

They embraced that edict with gusto and I laughed as a few of my mates fell off their seat into a flowerbed; we cracked jokes and sang along to the music that crackled over the loudspeaker. The more grog I consumed the cheekier I became. When customers left their car door open as they paid for their 'benzene' I'd hide in the back seat and yell 'BOO!' when they returned. Their reaction was priceless.

We left our spot at 9.30am and staggered along some ancient cobblestones into the entertainment quarter of the town. Along the way we passed posters that promoted the fight and I laughed loudly at the handiwork of an Aussie operative who'd used a texta to draw a Hitler moustache on as many photos of Beyer as possible. We marched on and I was pleasantly surprised to find a bar that was not only open but the owner was happy to accommodate a crew of Aussies who were obviously under the weather. As I settled back with a stein I noticed two freaked out hippies wander into the pub … they wore psychedelic clothes and looked as much out of it as I was. When I focused my bleary eyes I realised it was BG and Molly and I almost pissed myself laughing. They'd bought some far out 70s gear from a secondhand shop. Everything from that point is a blur.

I started drinking as soon as I returned to the hotel from the venue. It was not going to change the decision, or make it disappear; I just wanted to cut loose. I had such an empty feeling sitting there unrewarded, even though I'd flogged the world champion. I was so gutted, and so were the people who surrounded me. Nina was distraught and she must've said, 'Don't worry, Jack' (Nina's pet name for me) a million times. Jeff had bought a bottle of Veuve Cliquot champagne at the corner shop near our hotel in anticipation of the victory, but there was no way I could have touched it, the champagne would've burnt my palate that night because I felt so bitter. I went upstairs with Nina to fetch a two litre bottle of vodka we'd bought duty free to use for 'medicinal purposes', though I never imagined it'd be used to cure a broken heart. I phoned Chloe, and that really helped to pick me up off the floor. She had watched the fight on television and even though she had no idea of what had happened to me she was ecstatic. Who knows? She might have thought I was in a Wiggle's skit!

When I returned to my room the grog brought my emotions to the surface and I bawled. Nothing Nina said could stop me because it hurt like hell. If I had been beaten fairly I'd have copped it sweet, but being robbed blind in front of an international television audience was unbearable. I was so down I fell asleep with tears pouring out of my eyes.

Jack Cowin, who owns Hungry Jacks in Australia, had been kind enough to offer me the use of his private yacht that's permanently berthed in Europe so I could take some time out from the world after the Beyer fight. I have no doubt when he made his generous offer it was his intention that Nina and I would be enjoying a victory cruise. Sadly, it wasn't to be.

The skipper, Captain Phil, said it was up to me to plan the course — the Greek Islands, the Riveria or the Croatian coast which I was assured was beautiful. I didn't care where we went; I just wanted to somehow escape the hurt. When we walked down the long line of boats along the marina at Khafta I thought maybe Bill Gates was on tour because there was one that looked like an aircraft carrier — it was ours.

The opulence was mind blowing. At one place a television crew filmed our arrival because they thought it belonged to royalty; no Kings on board just two jokers in the shape of me and Bowdo. The four of us had an amazing time and it was one I'll never forget. While the scenery was beautiful, my head — and heart — just wasn't into it. All I could think of was missing out on the title … I couldn't escape the thought I should've been the world champion, and as much as I tried to fight it there was a crushing sense of depression around me. Nina could read my mind, Bowdo could sense my pain as did Louise and they tried to cheer me up. It was tough, and after five days I had to say goodbye to Jack's boat because I couldn't enjoy what was a wonderful gesture. I wanted to get home and deal with the setback by training and by working to get among the big boys.

CHAPTER 26

TOM McGUIRE
1918–2003

The Greenwood Pub, the meeting point where my family, friends and supporters gather in Perth to watch my 'away' fights on the big screen was packed when I fought Eric Lucas in Montreal for the WBC interim world title. There was, however, one bar stool with a well worn — and well loved — Green Machine T-shirt draped over it. While the stool may have 'appeared' empty to many of the people crammed in the pub, I know my grandfather, Tom McGuire was perched there in spirit and that he celebrated my triumph alongside a large number of the people who matter most to us. Pop ... Tom ... died two months before my bout with Lucas and his passing floored me, as it did my entire family. Pop and I had a loving relationship and even though he was in and out of hospital for the last two years of his life he remained a cheerful bloke who loved a joke as much as his clan.

He took a great interest in my boxing, too. My sister and a trusted mate named Jimmy Tranter took it in turns to drive

Pop to the Greenwood to ensure he saw my bouts while the owner of the pub — another good mate, John Hall ensured Pop always had the best seat in the house. It heartens me greatly to know my grandfather loved the fact my mates made a fuss over him by sharing a yarn and a cold drink before — and after — the fights.

An old merchant seaman, he was 'on deck' when I fought Markus Beyer in our first bout, and even though I lost in a controversial manner his pride in my performance humbled me.

One of my earliest memories of Pop is of him picking his four grandkids up in a big old yellow F100 Ford and driving us to the Atlantis Marine Park where to his constant nods and smiles of approval, we'd spend hours flying down slippery slides into what seemed like deep water. I remember him as a tall man — 6 foot 2 in the old Imperial measurements he always referred to, and he wore his hair slicked back in a distinguished manner. However, when he messed it up and took his false teeth out he'd scare the piss out of us all ... to this day I still don't know how such a good looking old bloke could create such a horrible look! It scared the heck out of us but God knows we kids loved it. We'd badger him to do 'the scary look' and when he'd give in we'd freak!

Pop was old school, too. He'd do such things as open the door for a lady and he'd look people square in the eye when he spoke to them. I'm sure he was proud his old-fashioned values rubbed off onto each of his grandsons. While Pop never spoke much about his wartime experiences, he served in the Merchant Navy on board the SS *Empire Hamble* during World War II. I understand he came close enough to the action to see the war up front but rather than dwell on those dark days he'd talk about anything else such as the footy, my boxing, Brendan's football and karate or how we kids were doing at school.

I was on en route to Russia to attend the WBC conference to pitch for a world title rematch with Beyer when he died, and it was a gut-wrenching time. The sense of loss was deep and it was compounded by the fact I was so far away from home. I shed plenty of tears unashamedly on hearing the news. While I'm not religious by any stretch of the imagination, Mum confirmed my belief that Pop would still watch me fight Lucas when she told me not to waste a second worrying that I wouldn't have Tom McGuire's support in such an important bout. She was adamant *nothing* would stop him from cheering me on. I believed her because in the lead up to the bout I could picture Pop sitting on his usual stool at the Greenwood with his hair slicked back and wearing his Green Machine T-shirt and trademark smile as the boys said 'G'day Tom'.

Pop's name, his birthdate and date of death were embroidered on the trunks and the robe I wore into the ring as a dedication to him. After I won the WBC belt my father … Tom's son-in-law … grabbed the robe and he planted a kiss on Pop's name. Dad's gesture didn't surprise me, they were close, but his spontaneous act of dedication made the victory even more emotional.

In the years that followed Pop's passing I knew he attended all of my fights and while that thought gave me strength it still hurt like hell not to be able to give him a hug.

CHAPTER 27

THE BRAWL IN MONTREAL

Fifteen minutes before I left the dressing room in the Bell Center Montreal to fight the rugged French-Canadian Eric Lucas for the interim WBC super-middleweight title my crew and I were dancing like drunken cobras. It seems crazy to think back upon it now but in the countdown to what was the biggest fight of my career outside of my title shot against Markus Beyer, we were jiving and clapping. Though, I had my reasons for it ... I needed to lift the tempo in the room after a small setback made the mood feel as if we were in a morgue.

I was hitting the pads to warm up when Jeff speared out a sudden jab and it tapped me on the nose. It wasn't a particularly hard jab but it was unexpected and within two seconds blood was spraying everywhere. I didn't want any evidence of the blood on my shorts or my body because I thought it would give Lucas some sort of a psychological advantage. I was also aware the few remaining minutes I had to prepare were ticking away so while I threw my punches I tried to suck the blood as it flowed from my nose. The whole thing was a distraction but what really annoyed me was the swing in the room's vibe. What had been light and jovial had suddenly become solemn and depressed. It was so quiet I could hear the guys chewing their gum faster and louder because they were nervous. I couldn't handle it so I let fly.

'It's only a bloodied nose for fuck's sake, fellas! I'm going out there to knock him out or get knocked out and you're worried about a bloodied nose? Pull your heads in and get it together!'

The boys didn't rally quick enough so I said anyone who wasn't prepared to dance for two minutes had to leave the room and they weren't to come back. It worked because each member of the Green Machine gang including Jeff, Dave Birchell, Steve Bowden, Henk Plug, Angelo Hyder, Molly, Billy Mead, BG and all the gang started to groove and jive, clap and sing. I joined in, swaying from side-to-side and laughing my head off. The ice had broken. So with all well in the world again I took a deep breath and walked out the door to face the highly favoured Lucas.

In all my fights I switched off the emotion the instant I climbed through the ropes and that allowed me to do my business but that wild night in Canada I was gripped by a surge of energy that was quite amazing. It started when I waited in the tunnel for the television director's cue to enter the ring. The crowd saw me and made it quite clear I was not welcome in their hero's town. The chants started. It sounded like rolling thunder at the back of the stadium and by the time it reached where I was standing it had exploded into a sonic storm of LUKE-ARR ... LUKE-ARR ... LUKE-AAR ...LUKE-AAR! punctuated by the massive din made by thousands of inflatable plastic clap sticks being whacked together. Insults were hurled from behind the relative safety of the metal barrier and security guards. I was spat on. Beer was thrown. It was ugly, feral behaviour but rather than feel intimidated and retreat into my shell as they had probably expected I remained calm and returned serve as I waited for the nod from the director. I pumped my fists in mock triumph, I clapped my hands in time to their chants and I smiled — broadly -at the sight of so many of them becoming infuriated by my 'stuff you,' approach. I walked to the ring with that smile plastered on my face. My smile wasn't one of arrogance or false confidence, it simply stemmed from a feeling of complete and genuine satisfaction that I was on the verge of winning the world title. By the time I climbed the three steps that led up to the ropes I was buzzing. When I climbed into the ring I felt as if my body was charged by a million volts of electricity, and all I wanted to do was to start throwing bombs at the former WBC champion who'd previously tangled with the likes of Roy Jones Jnr, Omar Sheika and Vinny Pazienza.

I needed to keep my guard up and my wits sharp against Lucas because he established a decent points lead in the opening two rounds. While I knew I was behind on the judges' cards I refused to allow any sense of panic to set in. I talked myself through the tough times. I can even remember thinking to myself if I didn't hurry up and pull my finger out

I'd be returning on the long flight to Australia in economy class with my head bowed low, feeling very sore and sorry, talking to Nina about what could have been and wondering how I'd be able to rebuild my career from such a loss.

With that Lucas speared out a punch; I saw it coming and evaded it easily. 'That was good, that was good, he just threw a good punch, you saw it and it missed you. You can do this, c'mon mate get moving.' I then connected a few good blows; I landed a few more and I suddenly pictured myself flying home in first class with Nina by my side and the WBC belt on my lap. I visualised both of us eating fine food, drinking nice hot coffee and watching the inflight movie in comfort.

It was great. The tide had turned. I teed off on Lucas frequently and accurately, landing solid right-hand bombs to his granite chin. I remember feeling his will and determination seep out of him. I knew I had to dominate him and I caught him with some lovely shots off the back foot and others as I moved forward. Towards the end of the fourth round I rolled under his right hook, and at the same time I threw a cracker of a right uppercut to his mid section, a punch that few people noticed, but, in my view, it was the one that marked beginning of the end for Lucas. I rate that blow as one of the best punches I have ever landed, and it's a view my dad wholeheartedly supports.

Indeed, that crisp uppercut was to have a dramatic impact on my life because seconds after delivering it I wobbled him with a left hook, and as the crowd fell silent, my corner went nuts. That was when the momentum shifted, because Lucas became the hunted. I peppered him for the entire fifth round, and Jeff was excited because, like me, he could sense the rugged Canadian had met his maker. Fenech yelled at me to go out in the sixth and finish him. His words will stay with me forever: 'Greeny, do me a favour. Go out there and hit him for three minutes and we're going home early.'

With that, I charged off the stool like a bull at a gate, and from the 'get go' I fed it to him. I didn't go wild; I just focused a series of accurate, calm but very aggressive shots at him. I brought him on to a crisp right hand that buckled his legs. My corner was exploding with anticipation of a victory and I heard them scream at me: 'You've hurt him, Greeny. You've hurt him!' I understood the next few seconds would decide my destiny — glory or what could have been. Now was the instant I needed all my skill and power to come together, and thankfully, they did not fail me. I landed an overhand right to his temple that forced him back up on the ropes. I then went to town on him. I could feel my fists sinking into his flesh.

Lucas was desperate to survive, to somehow fend me off to avoid getting knocked unconscious. I refused to let him breath. It was raw and primal, but it felt beautiful. During such moments in a fight, time seems to stand still, and it felt as if I was dealing him an eternity's worth of punishment as I hammered blow after blow. The referee prised us apart from a clinch, and I seized on the opportunity to put some distance between us. I landed a perfect uppercut, followed by a big left hook bang on the button, then a right to the side of his face that dropped him. Lucas was down on one knee; the ref pulled me from him and applied the count. I was in the neutral corner shaking as a result of the adrenaline charge that was surging through me. Then I saw Lucas do what no one thought they would ever see — he surrendered. His corner were on the ring apron waving the white towel. And that was it. Mission accomplished. The team was going home early. And I was returning as world champion.

CHAPTER 28

THE TWILIGHT ZONE

In boxing there is a saying that when you get knocked out or hurt bad you see the 'black lights', as in the black lights of unconsciousness. Some fighters say there is nothing worse than the void that envelops them from the instant they get knocked cold to the second they recover. Certainly nothing could match the hell I experienced during a fight in 2004 when I was trapped in a state of senselessness — a twilight zone — because of an extreme case of heat stroke. That night, against New Zealander Sean Sullivan at Perth's Challenge Stadium, I saw demons.

From the moment my Green Machine team selected Sullivan for the fight, an opportunity for my Perth supporter base to help celebrate my WBC interim champion victory, I knew it would be no stroll in the park. In his Pan Asia Boxing Association (PABA) title fight against Anthony Mundine a year earlier, Sullivan had not only taken Mundine the distance in their 12-rounder but judges from both sides of the Tasman believed the New Zealander deserved the points decision. I watched the bout and while it was scrappy I thought Mundine won. Regardless, Sullivan's record suggested he deserved my respect because apart from being his country's welterweight, middleweight, super-middleweight and light-heavyweight champion at various stages of his career, he'd won the IBF Pan Pacific welterweight belt in 2000 and unsuccessfully contested the Commonwealth title that same year. He'd forced top Aussie talent such as Sam Soliman, Nader Hamden, Shannan Taylor and Jeff Malcolm to go the distance. So I expected a battle. However, *nothing* could ever have prepared me for what would transpire. There were warning signs going into the fight but I wasn't prepared to heed them.

In Sydney nine days before the fight I feared I was suffering the first stages of a stroke. My tongue, lips, throat and chest swelled and I had an itchy, red rash that felt as if it was going to send me around the bend. I drove myself to Royal Prince Alfred Hospital in Camperdown and within minutes of my arrival to the emergency department the medical staff knocked me out for six hours and placed me on a drip. Despite numerous tests they couldn't work out what was wrong except to say it was probably a viral infection and because I seemed fine after I woke up they released me. Yet, rather than take the specialist's tip to rest and recover I foolishly returned to training and threw myself back into my complete routine, which included some gruelling sparring sessions. It was so bloody stupid because I didn't allow my system the opportunity to recover from whatever it was that had knocked me about. I have four excuses for soldiering on when I should've taken it easy, though none of them will probably make sense to most people. They included:

- My trademark pigheadedness.
- The fighter's instinct to not give up.
- I didn't want to let my hometown supporters down by cancelling the fight.
- I considered myself indestructible.

The 'bulletproof' aspect certainly played a big part in my decision to go ahead with the bout. It may have been I saw fighting Sullivan when I wasn't 100 per cent right a personal challenge to see if I was made of the so-called 'right stuff'.

What an idiot. To this day I have no clear recollection of the fight from the end of the fifth round; it's a fog. In the months that followed bits and pieces of the nightmare returned to me but even now, when I try to talk about my nineteenth professional bout, it's impossible to put it all together. What I can tell you is my brain felt as if it was broiling in a stew, my lungs may as well have been scorched by fire because it was so hard to catch my breath and, try as I might, as early as the fifth round I couldn't swallow water … actually, I was in such a bad way I didn't even want to take water. In hindsight, I probably made the mistake of whacking too much gel in my hair to keep it out of my eyes during the stoush because it may have trapped the heat that was generated in my head from the bright lights overhead. Allied with the existing viral infection it was a recipe for disaster. It was so hot some black Golden Palace.com lettering I had painted on my back literally melted off. At 4.30pm, the time we came out swinging it was 41.5°C in the shade. Inside Challenge Stadium the air-conditioning had conked out and the temperature in the ring hit a very dangerous 52°C.

By the end of some rounds, I was so disorientated I walked towards the neutral corner. As far as my performance was concerned Nina thought I looked dull and listless; I lacked what she called the usual 'Greeny spark'. Mum was scared for my wellbeing and all Dad could think as he watched me push myself towards the brink of disaster was if that type of effort was required to defend my world title he'd prefer for me to give the sport away.

In the seventh round I was panting as hard as a cattle dog that had just run 10 kilometres in the midday sun. While I really wanted to sit down during the minute break before the eighth round began I knew exhaustion would overcome me and I wouldn't be able to get back up to resume the fight. So I remained on my feet as Jeff Fenech yelled instructions in my ear. I doubt very much, though, if his words were even registering with me at that stage. In the days that followed the Sullivan bout many people were critical of Fenech's insistence for a KO victory. They'd wondered if he had become too obsessed with the KO so as to get one up on Mundine because he couldn't knock Sullivan out in their fight. I was perhaps only a decent punch away from being 'iced' but my competitive instinct, which was all I had left, wouldn't allow Sullivan to land it. Referee Brad Vocale stepped in to pull Sean and me apart when we were entangled in a clinch. When the 'third man' pushed me away I almost fell over. I flew back onto the ropes and when I was 'sling-shotted' back off them I managed to keep my Kiwi opponent at bay by landing two blows on him. Many people have said that I should have been ordered to move around and to jab out a couple of rounds to refresh myself instead of throwing non-stop punches. Sullivan took so much punishment the referee was looking at calling the fight off at the end of the fourth and fifth round. In my opinion, after watching the fight on DVD, I could have cruised through the last three or four rounds and won on points without jeopardising my health. (Looking back, I believe that would have prevented the onset of the exhaustion and dehydration).

When I 'came to' after it was all over, I was overwhelmed by a sense of humiliation and guilt. I couldn't remember anything of the last five rounds so I assumed I'd been knocked out in the tenth and that really hurt. When I was handed the mike, I apologised: 'I let my father down; I let my coach Jeff Fenech down; most of all I let my mum down and I let my little daughter Chloe down. But … but … but I tried my hardest … it wasn't meant to be tonight. There'll be a rematch, you can bet there'll be a rematch for sure. Thank you, Perth, thank you, Australia, it wasn't my night …'

My 'apology' would have been funny if the situation wasn't so serious. Even though I hadn't lost as single round I was in a very bad way. I started to vomit in the ring, was talking gibberish and my head felt like a furnace. I had lost eight kilos from my frame during the fight. The ringside doctor Noel Patterson was very concerned.

I was literally dragged back to my dressing room and I'm told a few of the boys had to push away autograph hunters and well wishers who seemed oblivious to my tormented state. Once in the room I just lay face first on the ground and was covered in ice, fanned with towels and wiped down with wet cloths. My body would jump as if I'd been hit by an electric shock; a journalist later described my body's involuntary movements as 'flopping around like a dying fish'. I drank litres of water but I couldn't keep it down. I was in such a delirious state it took Jeff, Billy, Dad, Nina and the rest of the Green Machine team 40 long minutes to convince me I'd won the bout. I experienced wild mood swings, which ranged from deranged fits of laughter to angry outbursts which frightened Nina because she thought I'd taken a bad whack to my head and I'd lost my marbles. My poor wife feared the mess she was trying to comfort was to be her lot in life.

At one stage, and I only know this through watching Mick Angus's documentary *The Fight Game*, I yelled at everyone to 'Get the fuck out. NOW! Noel get out. Dad you're here; BG that's okay. Nina. That's all.' Thankfully, Noel and the gang stayed until I could be rushed to hospital and placed on an IV drip. I spent the next ten weeks recuperating well away from the gym and boxing ring. In time I eventually regained my strength by eating well, spending time with my family and lazing by the ocean. To make light of a serious matter I signed off my text messages of thanks to my friends for their concern over the days that followed as 'Delirious Dan'.

When I reflect on that night a part of me is amazed — and, dare I say, proud — that I kept going. I'm extremely proud I had the will and the power to slog on. Some people, I know, will interpret such a sentiment as the height of stupidity but they should realise mine was a profession that required that type of mental and physical strength. Through that experience I learnt I could push through everything and anything, but I wasn't dumb. I learnt a lot from that fight and perhaps the biggest lesson was to never, ever place myself in such a precarious position again.

Some people have even blamed the after-effects of the Sullivan fight for my subsequent losses to Markus Beyer in our WBC world title rematch and my infamous defeat to Anthony Mundine. They thought I didn't look as sharp — or frenzied — as I did in my previous fights which resulted in 16 consecutive wins by way of KO. I don't know about that, but I have been told it takes the human body two years to fully recover from heat stroke.

CHAPTER 29

IS 'DAT' A GUN IN YOUR POCKET?

Before I sparred heavyweight bruiser James 'Lights Out' Toney in Hollywood's Wild Card Gym a few American fight types warned me that under no circumstance was I to be drawn into a toe-to-toe war with him. I'd end up knocked out — or worse. Toney, a world champion in four weight divisions, is cursed with a hair-trigger temper and has no semblance of self control. Some veteran sports journalists are too terrified to interview him face-to-face because they fear the wrong question will send him into a violent rage. One of boxing's cardinal sins is to intentionally hurt a sparring partner, but Toney has never had any qualms about belting or knocking them out regardless of their experience, size or weight. He justifies the brutality with a shrug of his broad shoulders and by saying he's merely helping to teach 'the craft' — and I still have the bruises to prove Toney did his best to teach this skinny Aussie a thing or two the day we boxed.

Despite being warned to avoid a bar-room style slugfest Lights Out and I could have staged our seven-round exhibition in a public telephone booth because pride wouldn't allow me to run. As for the big man, well, he *couldn't* run because he was too fat, some 40 kilograms heavier. I stood there and took the best he had to offer and in an act of madness I even invited him to take four free shots after he accused me of 'boxing European' which, in boxing, means you're scared of being whacked. It was dumb, but at the time it was a matter of pride. Our time together ended with Toney yelling for a member of his entourage named Kevin to 'go get my gun' because he figured I failed to show him enough respect. And it was no joke, he wanted his 'piece'! Thankfully, however, his mate refused to comply.

Toney and I started off on the wrong foot because I think he took offence at a harmless joke I made to one of his gang when he failed to turn up to a sparring session. He'd already left me posted on two other occasions, so by the third time I was *really* annoyed. I was in Los Angeles for some quality sparring and I'd turned down a number of good boxers to accommodate him. 'We can't fit James's head inside of the headguard because of the *steroids*,' I was told matter-of-factly by one of his entourage.

'What?' I asked, unsure if I'd heard him properly.

'Yeah,' he said. 'James is on the juice. We can't fit it [his head] in.'

Toney would eventually be stripped of the world heavyweight crown for drugs, but at the time I didn't care what he was taking. I was there to box — for a *third* time and he was not. So I said to his buddy as a joke: 'Look mate, tell James Toney if he doesn't turn up tomorrow I'm going to really turn his lights out.'

Well, Toney turned up bang on time and he was in a foul mood. He heralded his arrival by roaring and shouting abuse at no-one in particular but when he saw me the big fella stared daggers. If looks could kill I'd have been buried in Los Angeles that day. He was *filthy*. I thought it was a front so I winked at him and even laughed, but he remained as emotionless as an Easter Island statue. Until he found out someone was using what he called *his* toilet! 'GET THE FUCK OUT OF MY TOILET YOU FOOL! GET THE FUCK OUT OF MY CAN!' With that he smashed on the door and yelled more bloodcurdling threats. As I kitted up, I thought 'great he's in a bad mood!' but perhaps I should have paid more attention to the large amount of onlookers doing their best to keep out of the bloke's way. Even my coach was smiling at him politely during rounds.

I wondered why so many people had turned out to watch a little known Aussie spar? Then I realised I'd shot my mouth off and they were expecting to see Toney smash a smart-arsed Australian. I couldn't help but laugh at the latest crazy situation I'd placed myself in.

I'm pretty intense in most sparring sessions but this one was something else. I tried to use distance by spearing out the jab, but I didn't need more than a minute to realise even if I smashed Toney over his melon with a baseball bat it wouldn't have hurt him. Early in the opening round Toney unleashed a massive blow that should've removed my head from its shoulders. He followed that with a massive hook and for a few seconds I saw black. It rocked me, but the look on Light Out's face suggested he was shocked I hadn't hit the canvas in a crumpled heap.

Toney began to tire in the second round because of the excess pudding he carried around his belly. He started grunting and the noise was obscene. I placed my head on his shoulder so he couldn't punch me and said loudly, 'I'm sparring Porky Pig here!' He didn't appreciate the sledge, especially when those people within earshot started to laugh. His pride hurt, he unleashed the trash talk: 'Come here boy, come here!' To which I'd reply after throwing a punch, 'I'm still here mate, I'm still here!' Before the session I promised myself I wouldn't react to his insults or take them personally because the bloke didn't know me, and he certainly didn't know my family (to his credit he at least spared me from any disparaging remarks about my mum or Nina) but we soon got the in-ring banter going. Toney kept telling me how good he was and how lousy I looked. 'C'mon boy, c'mon paper champ … what have you got, bitch?' he'd say in-between punches. I was out punching him two-to-one even though the bombs I landed flush on his chin didn't make him budge. He squealed in delight at the sight of blood dripping from my nose: 'I'm painting him red! Look at that, I'm painting him red!' But I busted his lips up pretty bad and by the end of the session my back and shoulders were splattered with big blobs of blood from his own nose.

In the sixth round when Toney was leaning on the ropes and resting I threw three rapid punches and when he speared one back at me I fired a second volley and he was forced to retreat. It was the only time in the entire battle I managed to do that, but I treated it as victory of a kind.

In the seventh and final round I upped the ante by suggesting he should visit Australia because we had some 'good ol' cheeseburgers' and the tactic worked. He saw red and I gave him those four free hits. Looking back on it now I realise dropping my hands was downright stupid but his 'European' pissed me off. The important thing, though, I was still standing. My chin stood up to the test, proving it was rock solid and that not even the future heavyweight champion of the world could buckle it.

I was prepared to do ten rounds but Toney's trainer Fred Roach called a halt to proceedings. Toney was tiring badly, and I could have boxed all day at his sluggish pace. Toney wasn't happy about it. As I went through my warmdown he lost it: 'I don't give a fuck who you are, you're disrespectful'. Then he asked for his gun. I'd just given him a fair sparring session but he was threatening to kill me! Nevertheless, I decided Toney was a gang banger and I'd heard he'd shot up a few gyms in his time, so I gathered my wits and decided the right thing to do was to seek him out to shake his hand. But he wouldn't be placated. Uninterested, I waved him away and my parting words were for him to never come to Australia because he would not be welcome. And guess what? That shut him up. As I stormed off his assistant trainer Macka Foley looked me square in the eye and declared I was 'one tough muthafucka'.

Later that night we were at a steakhouse called The Ranch. We'd been there a few times and because the waiter knew I was a fighter from Australia he came to my table with a disappointed look on his face.

'It's a pity you weren't here an hour earlier, buddy,' he said. 'James Toney was in here, sitting at that table just over there!'

'Yeah, mate,' I said cheekily. 'A damn pity we missed one another.'

Above: My sister Narelle holds me tight for a family portrait. Sharni (right) behaved for the camera, Brendan is twisting my toes!

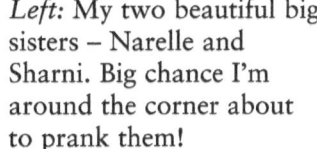

Left: My two beautiful big sisters – Narelle and Sharni. Big chance I'm around the corner about to prank them!

Left: Mum has been a constant source of love and support for all of us.

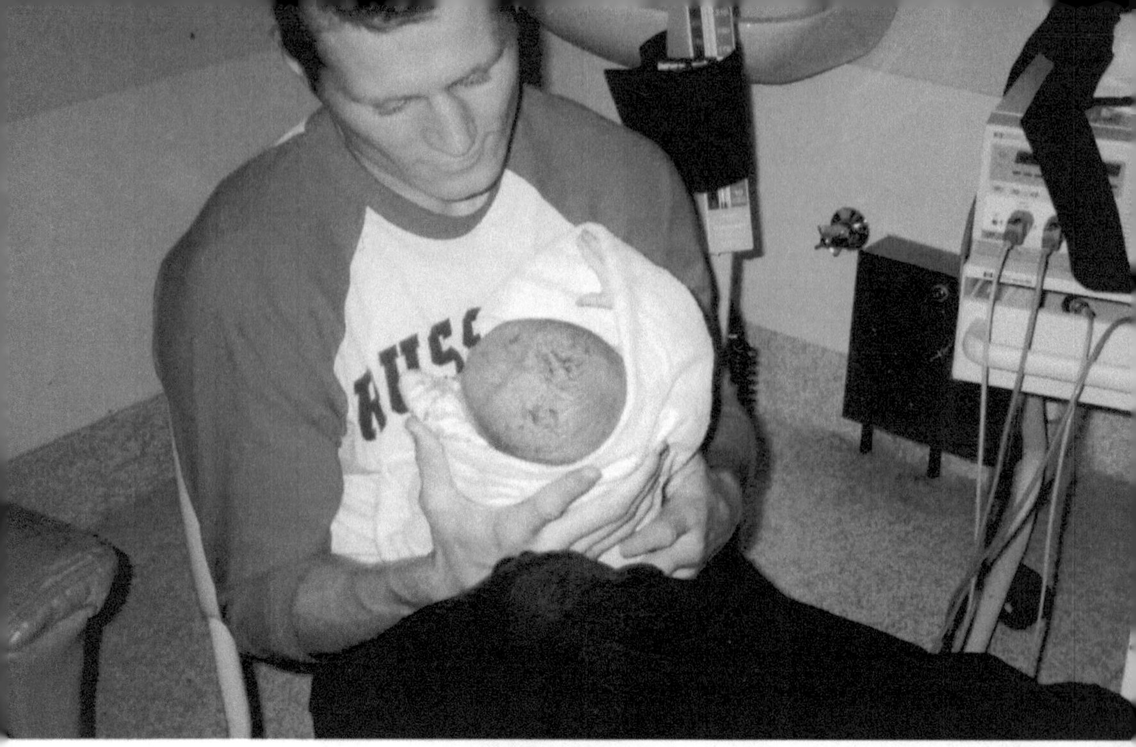

Above: 4 February 2002. Meeting my little angel Chloe for the first time. Her birth gave me an extra purpose as a fighter and a man.

Right: Bathtime with Chloe. Minutes after this photo was taken she fell asleep on my chest.

Right: At the race-track before my first world title fight in Germany with my own grid girl, Nina.

Chloe has me wrapped around her little finger. Here she is about to wrap herself around my neck.

My champ eight minutes into his journey. You would have needed a shovel to remove that smile from my face.

Right: They say little boys adore their mums but I think Nina's look of love proves it isn't one-way traffic as Archie ploughs through his daily sit-ups.

Below right: With hands built for destruction my kids are very secure in my man-made cradle.

Below: I am blessed to call these beautiful souls my family, and I look forward to our lives unfolding together.

Above: Archman's in safe hands with Uncle BG, who has fingers like rolling pins.

Left: Winners are grinners. My dad and I prepare for a loving embrace after my WBA world title triumph in Perth. This photo captures not just a father and son, but two best mates.

Below left: With Pop not long before he passed away – a gentleman to the end.

Below: Little Sophie Green. Always in our hearts.

Few have matched my mate Damian 'Damo' Scott for guts and determination. RIP little champion.

Celebrating the Socceroos 2006 World Cup campaign with the boys.

Taking a break from cracking heads to crack a few lips in the Maldives.

With Jeff McGlinn and my hulking XB. There's a fair bit of horsepower between the three of us.

Above: After a lazy day on the Indian Ocean with (from left) Molly, my cousin Chop, Wizza and Molly's dad, Lou. The beers went down a treat with the dhufish steaks.

Above: Benny O'Donnell, Brendan and me during our 'doomed' surfing safari following the Mundine fight.

Below: A petrol station became the best bar in town the morning after Beyer I.

Top: Most kids dream of going to the Olympic Games. In 2000 mine became a reality when I represented Australia in Sydney. (Peter Ward)

Above: Two great men I call 'brothers from a different mother'. Pat (on left) and Salas (on right).

Above left: One would be excused for thinking that this is the casting call for *One Flew Over the Cuckoo's Nest* sequel. These are pre-fight laughs, not tactics.

Left: The one and only Angelo 'H-Man' Hyder – the Three Stooges, Jackass, Benny Hill and Angelo Dundee rolled into one package.

With David Beckham in Sydney. He told me he was a mad fan of British boxer Ricky Hatton. *(Courtesy of Foxtel)*

Below: Steve Bowden and Bill Mead always had my back.

Left: Being photographed alongside 'The Greatest', Muhammad Ali during the 2000 Olympics was a great thrill.

Below: After 27 years, who'd have thought we would be steering our way to the top of the world. Me with my close mate Justin 'Molly' Molinikos.

Above left: My good friend Henk Plug. He's classic old school with a heart of gold.

Left: Hanging five with the great Sugar Ray Leonard during a trip to Los Angeles.

Above: Brooka, BG and Wizza – I'm proud you were in my corner, boys.

Below: From left to right: Craig Catterick, Steve McNamara, Hayden Knowles and Kevin Ivinns – the fast4football.com team – a stella bunch. We said we would do it.

Cop that Shagga. That kiss was six years coming – thank you, Arie.

Below: I love this photo. It captures the raw emotion of my world title victory in front of my home crowd, it also justifies why I did what I did – fight.

Punching power starts from the feet and strong legs are essential. A cool shot of a simple yet effective tuck jump. (Ian Regnard/Tungsten)

There is no substitute for hard work. My whole career has been forged out of my craving for it.

Above: On my way to my first world title. Rugged former world champ Eric Lucas tasting my power in front of 15,000 wild French-Canadians.

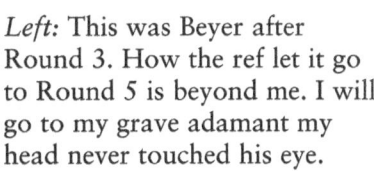

Left: This was Beyer after Round 3. How the ref let it go to Round 5 is beyond me. I will go to my grave adamant my head never touched his eye.

Left: 'Is that all you got?' Toying with the World Champion in my seventeenth Pro Fight. King Kong would not have beaten me that day.

Right: My most cherished moment with Jeff Fenech. Christmas came early in 2003 in Montreal when I beat Eric Lucas for the WBC interim world title. A beautiful, freezing December night when a dream came true.

Below: Argentina's Omar Eduardo Gonzales was the only man to ever put me on my arse in 16 years of boxing. His eyes were open when he threw the punch – so it wasn't lucky. (Carly)

Above right: On my way to nearly cooking to death. Serving it up to Sean Sullivan.

Right: Rattling tough American James Crawford just moments before putting him away.

Above: Landing a punch flush on Markus Beyer's chin in our rematch.

Top left: Mexican light heavyweight champion Kirino Garcia had a head as tough as his upbringing.

Left: Winning my fights not only gave me a surge of adrenalin that was addictive, but it also left me feeling invincible.

Below: Anthony Mundine evades one of my blows. I had other things on my mind during the most hyped fight in Australian boxing history – as well as the dodgiest haircut in the country.

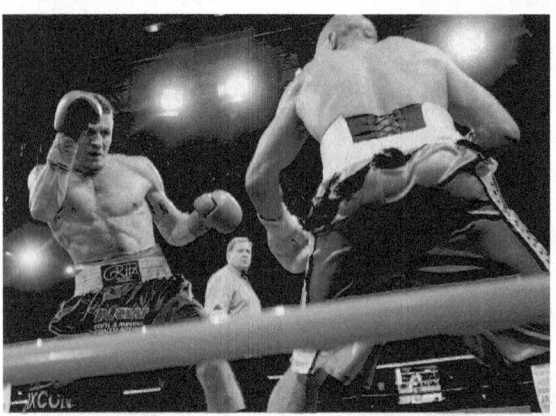

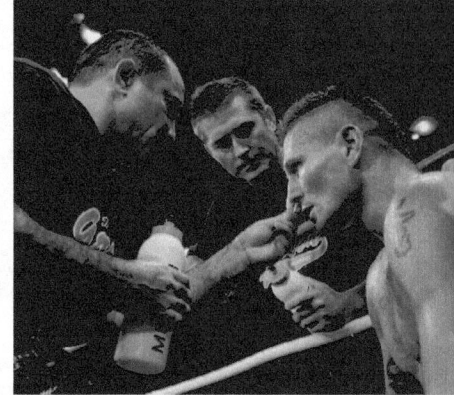

In the fight that gripped a nation, with millions of Aussies tuning in, Choc and I finally got it on. With no fuel left in the tank due to my wasting away to make weight, it was a very difficult night both physically and emotionally. My will and the meaning behind the pink band around my left arm ensured I marched forward relentlessly all night. My broken heart numbed the pain. However, we both had two fists – Mundine fired on the night, I didn't.

I've always believed the way a fighter returns from a heart-wrenching loss signals the mark of a true champion. I came back and made the long overdue step up in weight and demolished two Aussie world title challengers in Jason DeLisle (top) and Paul Murdoch (left and below). DeLisle took enough punishment for five tough men such is his warrior spirit. In 2005 and 2006, I was voted Best Puncher in the World for the super-middleweight division by the world-renowned *Ring* magazine. My power came with me in my step up to light-heavy.

Above: Smooth-talking American Otis Griffin's eyes say it all because, like a deer caught in the headlights, the end is near for him in our world title eliminator.

Above: After the hard work and sacrifice it's excitement overload after taking out Griffin.

Above: My final training session two days before fighting Croatia's Stipe Drews for his WBA crown.

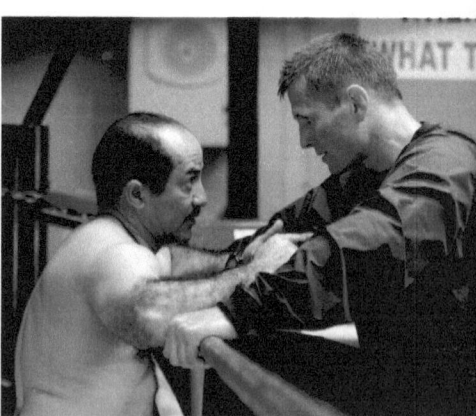

Above: Salas and I locked deep in game plan tactics for the awkward Drews.

Below: A place I will never forget – Challenge Stadium and my almighty supporters who gave me so much love and inspiration.

Left: Kermit the Frog with his game face on.

Below: The jolting power of my stiff left jab shocked Drews.

Below: I force-fed Drews my jab – the bread-and-butter of my arsenal.

I wanted to annihilate Drews from the get-go, and my aggression and intensity ripped the fight out of him early in the bout.

Drews did everything he could to avoid getting hit. I constantly rocked him with big shots despite his extraordinary height and reach advantage.

With my fists as hard as bricks I broke his will early in the fight with flush shots like this one.

I went nuts after the fight because I was overwhelmed by raw emotion on so many fronts. Led by Micky 'Whooska' Pember and Dave Birchell the team all sung along to John Williams's *True Blue* to celebrate. Being joined by thousands in the crowd made it a magic memory.

He ain't heavy, he's my brother. In a moment we will always cherish BG hoisted me onto his shoulders after I was crowned world champion. The satisfaction is also shared by my brothers-in-arms Salas, Angelo Hyder and Nathan Brooks. This photo will take pride of place on my wall at home.

CHAPTER 30

T FOR TERRIFIC

The one celebrity who struck me as being a great bloke — apart from Muhammad Ali — was the actor, Mr T. I am pretty nonplussed about people the paparazzi and media consider famous but when I was ringside at the Roy Jones-Antonio Tarver rematch at Las Vegas I was dumbstruck when I spied Mr T. I dropped everything to meet him. Nina thought I was carrying on like a groupie because I was yelling 'Mr T!' at the top of my voice. I was that excited. Rather than being a groupie I was revisiting my childhood because as kids Brendan and I were massive *A-Team* fans, and Sergeant B. A. Baracus ... Mr T ... was our favourite character. He played an ex-army commando on the run from the US government and we were captivated by his mohawk hairstyle, his tough talking and intimidating nature. We'd even try to imitate his voice.

Mr T, a kid from the ghetto in Chicago, changed his name from Laurence Tureaud by deed poll so everyone — rich or poor, king or conman — would have to call him 'Mister'. He has led a pretty amazing life. In his pre-mohawk days a bald-headed Mr T accompanied Joe Frasier into the ring for his rematch with George Foreman. Apart from Smokin' Joe he was also the bodyguard for such luminaries as Muhammad Ali, Diana Ross and Bruce Lee, and he'd skite about his service. 'Next to God, there is no greater protector than I.' Though, widely quoted for such sayings as 'When I was a kid we were so poor we couldn't pay attention' and 'The golden rule is he with the gold rules'. T was immortalised for his catchcry as Clubber Lang in *Rocky III*. The line followed a question in a press conference when he was asked if he hated Rocky. 'I don't hate Balboa,' growled Mr T. 'But I pity the fool.' I loved it but never thought to say it in a pre-fight press conference.

The second time I met Mr T was at the launch of *Contender,* Sylvester Stallone's reality boxing program. I made a beeline for him and asked if he could phone Brendan and hit him with what I described as 'some vintage T'. BG was working on a building site in Perth when his mobile phone rang, and I'm glad he had his safety harness on when he answered it otherwise he'd have probably fallen off the structure. 'Brendan,' Mr T huffed and puffed at his menacing best. 'I pity the fool! Grrrrrr!' Our childhood hero then proceeded to bombard Brendan with premium T and I could hear my brother laughing his head off from halfway across the world. He was ecstatic. That call made his day.

After Mr T handed my mobile phone back he asked something that blew me away. 'Did that sound good, man?' The guy is such a professional he wanted me to critique a prank call. 'Mr T,' I said. 'That was awesome. You are a legend!'

CHAPTER 31

DANNY DECKED

On the door of my fridge in my old Sydney base was the front page of a boxing magazine from October 2004. The headline screams 'DANNY DECKED!' and the photograph shows me plonked on my backside, the aftermath of a blow from Argentina's Omar Eduardo Gonzales. While I detest that shot, it served a purpose because whenever I went to the fridge in the build-up to a bout it reminded me to never, ever consider a fight — or an opponent — a gimme.

Gonzales deserved my respect on a few fronts. He'd fought for the WBF and IBO versions of the world super—middleweight titles and his record noted in 1999 that he'd enjoyed a unanimous decision over one of boxing's all-time greats, Roberto Duran. While Duran was 48 when they fought he was still competitive.

I'd had six months away from the ring before Gonzales and I shaped up to one another at Penrith in Sydney's west. But I'd been far from inactive. During my time off I trained in America, the highlight of which was my brawl with James Toney. While my training in the lead up to the bout was as professional as ever I'm afraid to admit in the back of my mind was the thought that Gonzales wouldn't be anywhere near the challenge of Beyer, Lucas and, although it was only a spar, Toney. It was a terrible case of poor judgement.

A few interviews I conducted before the bout highlight that I wasn't in the right frame of mind. I talked about a rematch with Beyer. I told Channel Ten's *Sports Tonight* it was my ultimate goal to retire from the fight game with all my marbles intact. In another interview I said I'd unify all the super-middleweight titles. It amazes me to think I treated Gonzales in such a way because I ignored my golden rule to never get ahead of myself and to focus fully on the job at hand.

After displaying plenty of ring rust in the opening round, I had a momentary lapse in concentration during the second. I dropped my hands for what was no more than a split second. It was enough time, however, for me to cop a flush punch and for the first time in my career I hit the canvas. Even though I bounced straight back to my feet before the referee's count even reached one my pride was bruised. It had been my aim to go through my career without ever being dropped but that was now blemished because I lowered my hands. I couldn't make up an excuse because regardless of whatever spin I might have put on it — like I was off balance — would've rung hollow. While I took control of the fight from that moment on and won by a TKO in the fifth round when Gonzales suffered a nasty cut on his eye lid, the knockdown annoyed me and it took quite a while for me to get over it. After the bout I told the crowd and pay television audience that I would learn from the experience. If every fight is, as I call it, 'a lesson', I learnt that night that a bruised pride hurts a hell of a lot more than bruised ribs.

CHAPTER 32

CAMPAIGN OF THE LOST

By 2005, my dream of a rematch with Markus Beyer had been realised. I was locked in to fight Beyer on his home turf where I'd have to again take on the politics and cunning that I believe had robbed me of the world title 18 months earlier. It wasn't the ideal scenario, but if I've learned one thing in life it is that you roll with the punches and make the best of any situation.

The controversial nature of our first fight ensured intense media coverage, and there were times when it was hard to focus on the business of training at Jeff's gym in Marrickville because cameras of all descriptions were constantly in my face, while reporters peppered me with questions about the 'headbutt'. I appreciated the attention, but I knew the only way I'd be able to properly prepare for my shot at redemption was to leave Australia. From the outset Jeff thought that was a terrible idea, and while he did his best to convince me to remain in Sydney, I refused to budge.

I again tapped Paul Miller on the shoulder to help me prepare for the fight as a sparring partner because he has a similar style to Beyer. It's funny, though I wasn't laughing at the time, but I don't think 'Mr Magic' has ever thrown a better left uppercut in his life than the one he unleashed five weeks out from my crack at Beyer as we sparred. It was an absolute corker, but it unfortunately left me with a badly mangled nose. It was the last thing I needed but rather than allow negative thoughts to take hold I told myself to forget about it — *it's only an inconvenience* — and to battle on. The fact is I wasn't sparring very well. A rift that had formed between Jeff and I deepened. When we landed in America I sensed Jeff was pre-occupied with other things. I soon discovered he had set the ball rolling to takeover as Mike Tyson's trainer. Mentally I was not in the best frame of mind because my trainer and I were not spending much time together on the eve of such a massive fight. On the contrary, Beyer by all reports, was powering along.

When I finally arrived in Germany it was 20 degrees below zero, *freezing*, and while it was so bitterly cold I was happy to be there because after a frustrating and often tense month on the road, Nina, BG, Dad and the gang were all there. However, my preparation remained on a lousy course. My training sessions were conducted in a room at our hotel, and it was far from ideal. I wanted to go to a local gym and train properly, but my trainer thought it would be a mistake to venture out in the cold, so we instead used a small room outside a sauna to move around in. It truly was a forgettable — and regrettable — build-up.

At the press conference I noticed Beyer seemed a lot more self-assured than he was before our first fight. He'd obviously done his homework, he'd prepared himself for another tough fight and he radiated confidence. It was a sign of things to come.

During the third round of my so called 'redemption bout' I did something I'd never before done in the boxing ring: I showed my opponent I was in pain. I have suffered broken bones in my hands, my nose has taken a beating and I've even suffered two smashed vertebrae in the ring but no-one ever knew about it until after I'd laid down my gloves. However, on this particular occasion when Beyer stung me with a massive body shot that crashed into my ribs, it hurt like hell. If Beyer had *meant* to do it I'll say this: he was bloody good because I reckon a sniper would've struggled for such pinpoint accuracy. He got me just as I released my breath and the result was maximum pain. I was angry with myself because boxing is a sport that is all about maintaining a poker face even if your whole world might be imploding, so I immediately responded with some punches to upset his rhythm, even though I was hurting badly.

A few things were becoming clear. Firstly, my days as a super-middleweight were coming to an end as I found I lacked energy as a result of the battle I'd endured just to make the weight limit. I was exhausted by the middle of the bout and no matter how hard I tried to hammer the 'go' button there was hardly any response. I was paying for the poor preparation. Unfortunately at this stage, Fenech and I were simply not clicking, so that 'walk through brick walls' connection we once shared in the ring as fighter/trainer was gone. Though I managed to unleash a pearl of a punch in the fourth round that wobbled the German, Beyer proved he was clearly in for the long haul by responding with some good punches.

He made that perfectly clear in the sixth when he caught me coming in towards him with a shot that sent my mouth guard flying through the air. In the seventh round he landed yet another stinging body shot, but I beat him to the draw with a crisp shot to his head that stung him. In the twelfth and final round I went for broke because I realised by remaining on his feet Beyer had done enough as the defending champion to retain his title. Though I had outpunched him two to one, my only chance at victory was to knock him out. My energy was well and truly spent, but my every instinct forced me to muster all I could for one last attempt. I literally charged out from my corner and landed a sweet punch that severely hurt Beyer and dropped him (the ref counted to six). Yet, while the champ was rattled he was also smart because like a drowning man Beyer clung to whatever he could to stay afloat — and that was me. He frustrated my ensuing raids by grabbing on to me and preventing me from pressing home my advantage. I believed he was only one big punch away from being stopped so I threw leather non-stop for the entire round, landing many good uppercuts and telling right hands. The atmosphere in the stadium was incredible, I could feel the combination of fear, anticipation and excitement oozing from the crowd and I lapped it up. It was like the Rocky

Balboa fairytale script...but I was living it, not watching it. I felt as if was only seconds away from a spectacular final-round world title victory, so it frustrated me no end that when the final bell sounded I was still trying to land that one knockout punch that I felt was still in me.

With one judge scoring the rematch a draw, another giving the result to Beyer by one point, and the remaining one giving it to him by three points, I often wonder whose hand would have been raised in victory had the fight been staged on neutral soil or if the fight had been held in Perth. However, to this day I don't hold any grudge towards Beyer at all. If anything my respect for him after our first fight had grown because he overcame a huge psychological hurdle after being beaten up so brutally by me. He proved why he was a three-time world champion by putting the memory of that hiding behind him. As far as my scorebook is concerned, though, it's one apiece.

CHAPTER 33

WILCANNIA

After Beyer II there were questions being asked about my future in boxing. While I certainly believed I had plenty left in me — another world title included — it seemed as if not everyone shared my belief. There were a few knockers but I didn't pay much attention to them because I've always trusted my own judgment. That said, though, I needed time out from the world to get my head together. To do that Dad and I took a road trip from Perth to Sydney. I'd recently bought a Ford 351 GTP from a good mate and long term sponsor, Denis McInerney, and I wanted to break it in. I figured apart from being an opportunity for Dad and I to see some of the world's most rugged countryside, the Nullarbor would also be a nice stretch of road to really open the motor up! During the three and a half days it took to cross the continent side-to-side, side-by-side. Dad and I covered plenty of other ground regarding my boxing future: my working with Jeff; my goals and my plans. It was exactly what I needed and together we worked out the steps that I had to take to get everything back on track. Our time together definitely helped my career path seem so much clearer. My dad is very special to me and I consider his opinion and thoughts very important. However, a detour to a country town that is a flyspeck on a map of Australia brought me face to face with a deep-rooted problem that generations of politicians haven't been able to sort out.

We were in outback NSW when I received a phone call from my mate and documentary filmmaker Mick Angus. Mick is one of those rare people who can talk on just about any subject and make sense. He is blessed with empathy and sincerity. During the filming of my boxing doco *The Fight Game*, we shared some quality moments together, one's I'll forever remember, especially some ultra competitive ping pong games that we believed had a definite Chinese-Taipei flair to it. At the time his partner Melinda was involved with the teenage hip hop group The Wilcannia Mob, a bunch of young Aboriginal kids who had a sleeper hit with their song 'Down River' after getting a real push on the ABC youth music station Triple J. When Mick found out Dad and I were near Broken Hill he asked if we'd drop by Wilcannia and say g'day to the local kids. Drugs, alcohol and petrol sniffing were big problems in the town, as was crime and vandalism. It was a fair hike out of our way, but Mick convinced me whatever time I spent in Wilcannia would mean something to the local community. I couldn't disappoint him, or them, so Dad and I agreed and turned the Ford around.

I didn't know what to expect but when I pulled up in the main street of Wilcannia it was like a scene out of *Mad Max*.

The place was like a ghost town. However, within seconds of stopping the car Dad and I were surrounded by kids on pushbikes. They lent inside the car window and pressed any button they could get a finger to on the dashboard. It was obvious they loved the look of the car and they wanted to see what it could do, so they dared me to do a burnout in the main street. I admit the idea was tempting but I resisted because I thought it would seem irresponsible. I asked them to point the way to community leader Brendan Adam's house and after being led on a wild goose chase we eventually pulled up next to a modest fibro house. Brendan had been inside enjoying a siesta and while he looked half asleep when he opened the door his eyes opened wide when he introduced himself: 'How ya goin' bro, when are ya goin' to beat Mundine?' He's my kind of bloke!

In the couple of hours Dad and I stayed in Wilcannia we met a lot of kids and they were great; they're bright, they've got spark and given half a chance I reckon they could do anything in life. People like Brendan are trying to offer Wilcannia's children direction but all the best intentions can't overcome the mind-numbing boredom these kids face *every* day. We could all do a lot more for these kids. Australia is a great country but people cannot be treated as they are in places like Wilcannia. The system can't continue to ignore them. While I am a retired boxer and not a diplomat or sociologist I challenge anyone who dismisses my views as a rant to go take a look at Wilcannia — or any other isolated township — and ask yourself if you'd like your child to be raised in that kind of an environment. My rival Anthony

Mundine — the self-proclaimed original Aboriginal — thinks he has a mortgage on the indigenous issue, but he is divisive. The pity of Anthony's outbursts, like calling rugby league selectors racists when an Aborigine isn't selected for a representative team, is he doesn't offer any solutions. He builds walls that have no purpose except to give *all* Australians something to hit their heads against. In the lead-up to our fight I was called a 'redneck' and a 'racist' by the more dim-witted members of his entourage. I turned up to the weigh-in with a mohawk haircut and an army jacket and was called a 'racist war mongerer.' It pissed me off at the time, but in the clear light of day their comments only proved they don't know me as a person. Indeed, I'd go as far to say *they* are in fact the racists by uttering such ignorant and unsubstantiated opinions about me.

On my return to Sydney I wanted to do something worthwhile for Wilcannia so I collected a lot of gear — gloves, punching bags, speedballs, that type of stuff — and sent them to Brendan. A few weeks later I heard the video games and pinball machines in the youth centre were gathering cobwebs because all the boys were boxing. That made me happy. A year later a bout I was scheduled to fight in Newcastle fell through, so it provided me with the opportunity to return. I dragged Mick along for the ride and after what seemed to be 500 cups of coffee later we were at the Wilcannia Bowling Club eating dinner with Brendan and about 30 locals, mostly Aborigines. It was a great night because we played pool against Wilcannia's champion; I talked boxing to a few of the diehards; a bloke asked me for

20 cents and when I gave him a 50-cent piece he brought back the change; a few ladies thanked me for making the effort to visit their town because they said no-one else had bothered with the place and the kids needed hope. It was a wonderful night.

The next morning I hosted a boxing clinic which kids from as far away as Broken Hill made an effort to attend. There is a lot of natural boxing potential in rural and outback Australia and I showed them how to use the equipment properly and tried to also correct a few punching techniques. However, I discovered the kids were happiest when they would put on a glove, run up and king hit their mate in the back of the head! Because they were belting each other pretty hard I had to put on my serious face and lay down the law: 'OI, GET HERE! CLOSER, GET IN CLOSER!' The kids went silent and looked sheepish as they herded around me. I noticed the elders were smiling because the kids were doing as they were told. 'YOU CAN'T KING HIT YOUR MATE! WAIT UNTIL THEY'RE LOOKING BEFORE YOU HIT THEM!' Well, when Mick heard that he almost fell to the ground laughing because, as he pointed out later on, it sounded as if I was telling the children it was okay to hit another kid if they were looking. For the record, kids, unless you're boxing, it's not cool.

I intend to return to Wilcannia again and next time I hit the highway to go out west, I reckon I'll take Nina, Archie and Chloe along with me. I think they'd take a lot from the experience, and I know the women and girls of the township would be happy to see them and talk to them, too. So, thank you to the beautiful people of Wilcannia for making me feel so welcome with your warmth and giant smiles. But like so many other places in Australia, the odds are stacked against them. Unfortunately that will continue to be the case until Australians of *all* colours and creeds realise we're all in this together.

CHAPTER 34

JEFF FENECH

When I won the world title from Stipe Drews I thought to thank Jeff Fenech in my acceptance speech. Even though Jeff and I had split in a less than amicable way, I wanted to thank him for the role he played in my professional career as my trainer. Jeff interpreted that acknowledgement as an opening to train me again but that was definitely not my intention.

As a young Jeff Fenech fan I knew the rhyme and rhythm to each of his fights off by heart. I was so familiar with them I'd annoy the crap out of my mates whenever we'd watch the old fight tapes because I'd give them a 'heads up' on what was about to happen seconds before the 'Marrickville Mauler' unleashed a wicked combination or delivered a blow that put an end to the fight.

'Watch this, boys,' I'd yell. 'Jeff leads with the right, here, watch, keep watching … here it comes!'

Looking back on it I guess my telegraphing everything of interest Jeff did in those fights must've taken the excitement out of the experience for the boys. However, I just couldn't help myself; I'd get so excited. Back then I thought Fenech was Australian boxing. It was my dream to follow his footsteps and become champion of the world.

As I progressed through the amateur ranks I'd travel to Sydney from the Australian Institute of Sport in Canberra to spar with the guys from Team Fenech. I really caught Jeff's eye before the 1997 Australian amateur titles. I'd only had 16 bouts, but I iced one of his fighters with a big right hand. I continued to train on and off at his gym in the build-up to big fights and benefited from the experience. After a tremendous spar with Glen Kelly just before the Sydney Olympics I was ecstatic when Jeff suggested I join his troupe of professional fighters. It pleased me a lot and I couldn't think of anyone better to fight for than a former world champion I'd admired for his guts and determination.

My natural, aggressive style and eagerness to please Jeff meant we clicked from the outset. I trusted him to guide me through what were uncharted waters — professional boxing. When I look back on it now the style of coaching and tactics Jeff employed showed that he wanted me to emulate his style. I didn't mind that then. I followed him blindly and faithfully. If Jeff said to jump, I'd ask how high. My eyes have opened since then and I think some things should have been done differently.

On the flip side, I think Jeff couldn't believe his good fortune to have found a fighter who had power in both hands, a solid chin and someone who embraced the style of fighting he preached — to go forward, apply pressure and knock the opponent out at all costs. Such an approach almost cost me my life against Sean Sullivan in 2004. Yet, even although I had doubts about the way my trainer handled that fight, I remained loyal and defended Jeff from his critics when they bagged both the fighter he was trying to sculpt and the tactics he employed. People who knew boxing were critical that it was OK for Jeff to fight the way he did because he'd been in the lighter 54-57kg division, meaning the damage he sustained was nowhere near as intense as what I copped in the 78-83kg class. Walking forward on a bigger man is detrimental to your health, and it was something that could not be sustained over a long period of time. While I accepted the sense in the critics' argument my loyalty wouldn't allow me to entertain the idea of contemplating the offers I received from other trainers.

When Jeff and I trained one-on-one I was always focused and I did everything possible to impress him. In those sessions I felt myself improve as a fighter and I loved the pad work we did together. The highlight of our association was the night I defeated Eric Lucas for the WBC interim world title in Canada. It was great to share that sense of achievement with Jeff. It was magic. All of our hard work and sacrifice had paid off. It was a far cry from the Beyer fiasco. To have knocked out a former world champion to win the title was a dream. That night will live in my memory forever, and I mean it when I say having Jeff in my corner made the moment even more enjoyable. Words can't describe the sense of camaraderie and pride I shared with Jeff that freezing December night.

After Lucas, a series of cracks formed in our relationship. The Sullivan fight took place and I suffered heat stroke and came close to dying. I put in a dog of a performance against Omar Gonzalez when I was knocked down for the first — and only — time in my career. But the most damaging of all was Beyer II — the rematch I'd so desperately craved. That fight was a long time coming but in the meantime I'd secured a WBC title defence against the Danish super-middleweight star Mikkel Kessler when I beat his promoters in the purse bid to host the fight in Perth. Jeff took issue with my involvement in the bid process because he thought I risked losing my focus. I was merely trying to protect myself and ensure the negotiations were done properly, professionally and successfully. The fight didn't go ahead. Kessler fought Manny Siaca for the WBA belt five weeks after the purse bid and he won the crown. While Kessler and I didn't cross paths, I at least realised I knew how to negotiate successfully. It opened a new world for me, I was able to control my own destiny.

Encouraged by my success with the Kessler negotiations I oversaw the purse bid for Beyer II. It was a game of smoke and mirrors because Justin and I told select people what we were offering to host the bout. We told them numbers that were way below what we intended to offer because we knew they'd tell the Germans. Justin and I calculated the maximum we could bid through my company Green Machine Promotions without being forced to sell the house I'd recently bought in Perth. We lost the bid to host the fight in Western Australia by an agonising $US34,000 but the $US2.15 million Beyer's people were forced to pay was a record for a super-middleweight world title. I also took some solace in knowing the narrowness of the bid loss proved I understood the money side of the business and that my previous success with the Kessler bid was no fluke.

While I didn't win the purse bid I was determined to flog Beyer and figured the best way to give myself every possible chance would be to leave Australia to train in Los Angeles. I was worried the controversial nature of my loss to Beyer would be fodder for the media and I didn't want my focus on anything but defeating the German. Jeff disagreed. He was adamant we should stay in Australia, but I insisted we were bound for the US. That was the first of many disagreements we had in the weeks ahead. In hindsight, I concede my decision to base myself in LA was not the best move. However, once we landed in America Jeff hooked up with his friend and former world heavyweight champion Mike Tyson and he was busy with him. The more time he spent with Tyson the more I worried Jeff had things other than my world title shot on his mind. I arranged my own physiotherapy, massage, injury rehabilitation and chiropractic sessions. Some people might shrug their shoulders at that and say 'so what?' The boxer's job in the countdown to his bout is to concentrate solely on the business of fighting — not tracking down a chiropractor and organising a driver to navigate his way through one and a half hours' worth of traffic to repair an injured elbow and back.

Unfortunately, the extra load I had to carry made it difficult to focus on the job that awaited me in Germany. Adding to my stress was the fact I was not performing as well as I'd have liked in the gym and sparring ring. Five weeks before the bout I copped a badly broken nose courtesy of Paul Miller. I asked Paul to accompany me to America and then on to Europe because he replicated Beyer's style, perhaps a little too perfectly. Yet a more serious problem than my banged-up nose was that I didn't click with Jeff when it mattered most. I'm certain any fighter who has been in that situation will understand when I say it was difficult to concentrate and remain upbeat. When I look back on that time I'm absolutely dumbfounded that Jeff and I only viewed my first fight with Beyer together the week before the rematch. Yet, even after we watched the tape, Jeff didn't have a lot to say. He simply said something along the lines of: 'You've got to smash him. You know what to do.' I was disappointed. It was a far cry from the first time I went to Jeff's house in 1995 and we watched hours of his fights on video. He had me count and mark down the number of punches he threw during each round so he could tally up his punch stats.

We flew to Germany but Jeff and I didn't spend much time together. He had his group of people; I had dad, Nina, BG and some mates. I walked into Jeff's room one afternoon in Germany and he was watching Mike Tyson fights on video. Sure, we'd talked about the fight and what I needed to do once it started but I would have preferred to have found him watching Beyer. We didn't go to a boxing gym to train because Jeff didn't think it wise to venture into the cold. Instead we trained in either a hotel room or on slippery tiles in a 3 x 3 metre change room outside a sauna. When I started training with Ismael Salas I learnt to appreciate the importance and benefit of training in a boxing ring and a proper boxing environment.

At 6pm on the night of the fight I was sitting in the room alone when Jeff dropped in and told me he had to go because he said the nerves were doing his head in and he couldn't sit still. My trainer said he had to go to the venue to calm himself down. What could I say? Word eventually reached me that while I was sitting solo Jeff was in the crowd watching Bob Mirovic fight Timo Hoffman where he yelled out instructions to Bob. I later heard rumblings that Mirovic was viewed as a possible opponent for Tyson — who was to be trained by Jeff — in his comeback bout. In my opinion, the trainer and fighter should have been together in the hours leading up to a world championship rematch. Mirovic lost his shot when Hoffman triumphed by a unanimous decision, albeit a dodgy one. While I didn't know that at the time, I remember feeling funny when my dad and BG asked me where Jeff was when they found me sitting alone in my room. Telling them raised a few demons in my mind. In my heart of hearts I knew my trainer should have been with me.

Ten minutes before the fight Jeff hurled obscenities at Angelo Hyder in the dressing room over an issue that should have been sorted out in private. It took away the focus of everyone in that room. It was an unnecessary distraction before going out to fight for a world title. It sucked. However, I'm certain the pressure and strain of our relationship was what tipped him over the edge on that occasion.

I lost the fight. Beyer retained his belt. I went back to the dressing room, and it was all very grim. Jeff left for the hotel while I did my drug test. When I walked through the bar area I noticed him drinking with a group of people that included Don Majeski. I was glad Don was on deck because he had clout in the WBC. Jeff later told me the New Yorker secured me the No.2 ranking because, despite the loss, he pointed out to the WBC officials that the fight was very close and the ending dramatic. Fenech told me he was headed to America the next day, and we'd sort things out back in Australia. With that I went upstairs with my family and friends, people who were there for me at a time when I really needed them.

I left Germany for Perth the following day and I felt gutted. The loss had hit me hard. The toughest part was the feeling of distance between Jeff and me. I had a strange feeling in my stomach. After eight days of hearing nothing from Jeff while he was with Tyson I phoned him. We had a short conversation where nothing of any note was said. A week later I heard he was back in Sydney so I booked a flight and caught up with him at a coffee shop in trendy Leichhardt. We got a few things off our chest. Jeff made some valid points. He thought my decision to train in Los Angeles was wrong. He thought I'd made a mistake by allowing too many people in the change room before the fight. He explained he'd given Tyson his word that he'd help him train, but added it was highly unlikely Iron Mike would fight again and he'd be back in Australia as soon as I was ready to resume training.

I was happy we'd aired a few differences. I returned to training and because I hadn't heard from Jeff I gathered he'd made the decision that he wanted to align himself with Tyson. When I called Jeff two weeks later he was in Los Angeles and admitted he'd been dreading my call. He told me Tyson was training the house down. That revelation shocked me because I saw him struggle to complete two rounds of pad work before I fought in Germany. However, Jeff explained Tyson had presented him with an opportunity to set his family up financially. He suggested I relocate to America to train with them, but there was no way in hell I was going to try to rebuild my career by relocating my family to Phoenix and play second fiddle to Tyson. I told Jeff that I did not begrudge him his decision to do what is best for his family. I wished him luck because in my heart of hearts I figured he was going to need it. Rather than feel abandoned by my trainer I cut my losses and looked for other options.

I eventually linked up with Cuban-born, Thai-based Ismael Salas. After I told Nina, Dad and Brendan of my decision, I thought the decent thing to do would be to inform Jeff to save him from reading about it in the papers. He seemed stunned by my news and simply said something along the lines of, 'Oh, OK then.' But I was moving again — and in the right direction.

Mike did box under Jeff in June 2005, but it was a sporting tragedy. With the great Muhammad Ali sitting ringside Tyson refused to get off his stool for the seventh round of his bout against the unheralded Irishman Kevin McBride. I saw it as an inglorious end to the career of a man who once instilled fear throughout the boxing jungle, a man who was once one of the greatest heavyweights of all time, whom I used to watch in awe.

Since Jeff and I have gone our separate ways he hasn't had too many positive things to say about me, not that I have any need for them. Sometimes I look at photos of us together, and I think of the good times, and there were many. But I sleep well at night; content in my heart that I was loyal to the end and I conducted myself with dignity.

CHAPTER 35

SALAS

When Jeff Fenech and I split, I needed to find a trainer — and quick. While there was no shortage of locals offering their services I wanted somebody who could take me to an extra level. However I want to stress that even though my relationship with Jeff was in freefall for quite some time, I waited for a replacement. I accepted Jeff's decision to help Tyson get his career back on track as the last rites were being read over our arrangement.

So I began to cast a wide net to find the right trainer. I was 32 and had no time to waste. I needed to find someone whom I could totally trust, someone I believed would make the right call if my world was falling apart in the ring and a person who I believed would look after my wellbeing at all times, a person whose sole priority was to train me. The person I hooked up with also had to be someone who was prepared to put his entire efforts into me at the expense of his own ego or profile.

It isn't easy to find someone who can live up to such expectations — especially in a sport like boxing. The traits I demanded were more like those of a saint than a trainer. It was important, however, to set a high standard because the relationship between a fighter and his trainer is perhaps the most complex of any in sport. It can be a tinderbox that needs only the tiniest of sparks to set it off. In the lead-up to a fight the boxer goes through physical and mental hell. He's always hungry, he trains through exhaustion and little things that would normally not even rate a blip on his radar suddenly aggravate him. Sometimes the fighter explodes and he'll channel his rage and frustration at his trainer. I can lose it at times in the gym, but any anger is always directed at myself, no one else.

Justin Footit, a bloke I went on a few boxing trips with early in my amateur career, alerted me to Ismael Salas via a few emails he'd sent while in Japan. When he travelled abroad Justin would keep in shape by training at local gymnasiums, and that's how he met Cuban-born Salas. His emails painted the portrait of a bloke who definitely knew the business of boxing and a fair bit about life. Justin cited the fact that Salas not only had some wonderful training techniques but also that he emphasised the need for all of his fighters to possess a nice, stiff left hand. That struck a chord with me because it's my philosophy. Forget flashy hands, the straight left is every fighter's bread-and-butter punch. I'd actually read about Salas two years earlier in the local boxing magazine, *The Fist*. I did my research and discovered he had trained five world champions. In 1996 he was named the

WBA's trainer of the year. He'd travelled the world as coach of the Thai, Kenyan, Pakistan, Japanese and Dutch national squads. He'd coached Cuban super-heavyweight Felix Savon who won Olympic gold medals at Barcelona, Atlanta and Sydney. The more I heard the more I liked. I phoned him at his home in Bangkok and by the time we finished speaking I'd decided to fly to Thailand that night to meet him to see what he could offer my career.

Within 18 hours of hanging up the phone I was at Bangkok's international airport. The first thing that hits you is the humidity. The second thing that hit me was Salas. A little ball of muscle ploughed through the crowd calling my name. He was nuggety, closer to 50 than 40, sharp-eyed and serious looking. He reminded me so much of my first trainer, Pat. He was a father of eight. Three of his kids — Joy, Junior and Gina — are to his Thai wife and I could tell by the way he spoke that his family meant the world to him. I liked that because it gave us something in common other than boxing. We spoke at great length over a meal of Thai red curry chicken, and I agreed with his views on training and fighting.

Salas was at my hotel bang on time the following morning and took me to a Muay Thai gymnasium owned by the city's police chief. The gym was a place for warriors. It was primitive, with well-worn bags, dripping taps, grey concrete and dirt. The fighters who trained there were tough and, when they punched or kicked there was intent in each blow because they were literally fighting for a feed. I also noted the respect Salas, an outsider to their culture, commanded. Before I put my gloves on Salas did something no trainer had ever done with me. He sat me down and spent the next 20 minutes wrapping my hands nice and tight. The fighter's hands, he explained, were to be respected because they are the tools of the trade. He bound them as an artist would mix paints and that made a positive impression. We then did some pad work together and it all felt right. He liked my power and aggression. I liked his approach. Salas had great philosophies that impressed me. 'Have a cold mind, hot heart', was one that carried great weight.

We trained together for four more days and by the end of my stay I phoned Nina and Dad to announce I had a new trainer. Salas came to Australia eight weeks before my fight with the American James Crawford and one of the first things he did was treat to my hands. My hands get very sore as a result of the punishment they've been subjected to over the years. It can be very hard, sometimes near impossible, for me to tie up my shoelaces. To help improve my hands Salas introduced me to an old Cuban remedy. We bought a large old pot from a second-hand store and some paraffin oil to mix with candle wax. Salas boiled the concoction and placed the steaming pot next to a bowl of ice. I formed my hand into a fist and plunged it into the formula, drew it out and allowed it to set. I peeled the film off, threw it back into the pot, and then stuck my hand into the ice. The extremes in temperature allowed the circulation to start moving. The result was outstanding. Sometimes I follow that routine four times a day and it has done wonders for my hands.

After my victory over Crawford there was criticism from outsiders that Salas had tinkered too much with my style by having me fight off the back foot. They said my strength, my aggression and power were my big-ticket items. They didn't much like the new-look Green Machine. They preferred the walk-up style, the style that made me a target for Beyer in our rematch. While some tried to crucify him, I appreciated everything Salas had done because he prolonged my career and spared me from unnecessary punishment. In the time we were together I reckon there was a 70 per cent decrease — at least — in the amount of 'damage' I suffered during a fight. The walk-up style the critics longed for was not good for me and I still can't fathom why they would have thought it was a bad thing for me to step back to avoid being cracked. My performances in my earlier fights might have given the impression my head craved leather. Well, it didn't. I had instead developed a style that never took a back step or let one go through to the keeper. Salas has been embraced by my friends — and fight fans — as a gentle, humble and honest man. I speak perfect 'Salasanese' so I have no trouble understanding him. He taught me some Spanish phrases so we could communicate during a bout. The English phrase he would use during a fight, and it cracked everyone up, except perhaps my opponent, was a line from an Al Pacino movie *Scarface*: 'Say hello to my little friend.' In Salasanese that means 'Throw a good, straight left jab, Danny'. He screamed it out during my fight against Paul Murdoch just as the Melbourne crowd fell silent, and those who heard it in the front rows pissed themselves laughing. I guess fight fans don't expect to hear that type of thing from a boxer's corner.

CHAPTER 36

THE ELECTRIC EELS

Fuifui Moimoi is regarded as one of the hardest running forwards in the National Rugby League competition. The Parramatta Eels player is 183 centimetres tall and he hits the scales at an imposing 105 kilos and I can vouch *every* ounce of it is rippling muscle. Fuifui's job is to cart the football up into the jaws of the opposition's defensive line, and while I don't quite understand league his role seemed akin to running headfirst into a brick wall. Yet, more often than not it's the opposition defenders who finish second best when Fuifui charges into them. He is a Tongan terror, and as part of a power specific fitness programme developed for me in 2006, I wrestled Fuifui — and a few of his team-mates — at Parramatta Stadium. He's strong, *bloody strong*, and I didn't always follow the rules when we locked horns because he has a whopping 25 kilos on me! The first time we were matched up and I gave Fuifui a good swift punch to the guts when I was pinned in an awkward position. I wanted to see how he'd take it and I was shocked to hear the big bloke say in a high pitched shrill; *'Nooooo punching, Dann-ee!'* He's a monster of a man and I would never have imagined he'd be such a softly spoken and gentle guy.

I was also thrown in to wrestle with another Tongan tornado named Feleti Mateo and I found it to my advantage to grab him by his afro hair and drag him to the ground. One young footballer who really impressed me was Jarryd Hayne. He was only 17 when he was given the tap on the shoulder to wrestle me. The club had raps on him but from what I gathered there were concerns he didn't train hard enough. He was a winger, and the other players, like Mark 'Piggy' Riddel told me that was the domain of the code's 'pretty boys' but Jarryd put up one hell of a fight ... he had a massive competitive streak because he dug deep. It didn't surprise me when he starred in his debut on the wing for NSW in the 2007 State of Origin series against Queensland. For people who live in non-rugby league states Origin is 80 minutes of bone-on-bone savagery and the then 19-year-old Jarryd didn't only survive, but he thrived. I am no expert but his performance in the toughest form of league suggested he was a superstar in the making.

I was fortunate enough to train alongside the Eels through my relationship with Hayden 'H' Knowles and Craig 'Cat' Catterick; Parramatta's strength and conditioning staff. When they weren't helping the Eels try to fulfill their goal of a premiership, H and Cat worked in conjunction with Salas to help get me in the best possible shape for a fight. We joined forces soon after Jeff and I split. I needed to assemble a professional team to help me reach my career goals and I was prepared to cast a wide net to recruit the right crew. Wayne Loxley, a member of Green Machine Promotions also worked for Athletics Australia and it was he who advised me to contact Hayden, a highly regarded shot putter in his youth before he focused his attention on sports science. Hayden and Craig's enthusiasm and attention to detail was so thorough it made me want to blow their minds every time I trained. H tried hard to refine my technique to attain more power and his — and Cat's — positive attitude rubbed off on me. They formed Fast4Football.com and they adopted a scientific, yet very specific approach to the business of getting people fit. People often queried my new training methods, many were ignorant by scoffing that pumping iron would offer a boxer no benefit. Those critics didn't realise H and Cat were actually improving my explosiveness and the power in my punching technique. They were increasing my speed and agility and working in conjunction with Salas to prolong my longevity in the sport. They weren't trying to turn me into a powerlifting rugby league player. While neither professed to be boxing experts I was impressed by how they prepared NSW-based heavyweight Kali 'Checkmate' Meehan for his WBO world title shot against Lamon Brewster in 2005. While I believe Meehan was robbed blind by the judges, his ability to throw punches from go to whoa was an awesome effort by a big man. His ability to punch on when he would normally have grown tired was a testament to Craig and Hayden's devotion to duty.

It surprised me to learn from Hayden in our first telephone conversation that he had some doubts about his being able to help improve my fitness. He was dubious because he'd watched me do my weights with Jeff once and thought it was too old school. Hayden noted the programme I followed under Fenech did little for the explosiveness I needed as a boxer. While Hayden clearly respected Jeff's reputation as a champion fighter, he dismissed my weights sessions as nothing more than a series of toning exercises. He was concerned about my attitude towards training. I'm pretty confident I KO'd those concerns in the early stages of our relationship. It wasn't what I expected to hear, but when Hayden and Craig realised I wanted to increase my punching power — and to improve my agility so as to extend my career's longevity — they were keen to help. They realised for me to attain maximum power in my punches I needed to be able to generate that from my feet and transfer it through my legs, hips, shoulders and fists. They designed a series of movements to help me achieve that. Through the boys I assembled a remarkable team of people who provided me with an edge in the ring. Dr Steve McNamara — aka Dr Death — is not only Australia's leading respiratory expert but a champion bloke. There were occasions when he arranged for the MRI centre to open for me at 6am and would not have thought twice about sending in a chopper to pick me up from training if it meant an injury could heal quicker! Kevin Ivinns was my chiropractor who worked over and beyond the call of duty when I needed him in Sydney. Nothing was ever a drama for big Kev, as he'd quite often come out late at night to fix me up, and apart from getting greats results I liked that he always had a smile to boot. In Perth my good mate Noel Patterson is my chiropractor and he has kept me in tip-top shape for nearly 10 years. Noel was there for me those times when I could hardly move, and within days, I felt like new. I would probably need a walking stick if wasn't for him! Whilst in Perth my childhood friend Jeremy Hunter oversaw my physio and any rehabilitation I needed in my downtime. 'Jes' and I have been mates since we were nine and he has pulled me out of some deep holes by using his expertise to diagnose and treat some wicked injuries. Most of the times it was done over a coffee with a golf lesson from his cracker of a son, Max.

Cat, who was a policeman and a paramedic before becoming a top conditioner, had a multi-faceted role as my masseuse, physio, occasional wrestling dummy and exercise technician. For a bloke pushing 45, he is a machine! He often towels up the Parramatta players in fitness drills — and often he took on more than one player at a time. A stellar bloke, Craig never once uttered the word 'no' to me — and, believe me, I have put him on the spot more times than I could ever hope to remember. He also took care of my supplements by providing me with an extensive array of Musashi products to assist in my recovery and sustenance. He also hooked me up with Victor who've supplied me with thousands of metres of plaster tape to protect my ankles and the tools of my trade — my fists. *Painaway* has also kept me in the game, providing me with much needed anti-inflammatory spray and cream. Few people know I fought my entire seven year professional career with four broken and chipped bones in my right hand. It was agonising but I found *Painaway* eased the pain and allowed me to soldier on.

Hayden is a real gun and was the brain's trust who mapped out my programme. His attention to detail was astonishing, second only to his enthusiasm. Every opponent presented new challenges, and Hayden always thought outside of the box when conjuring up plans to help me overcome them. His passion was contagious and it made me want to blow him out of the gym every time we trained. I used to rave to him about the joy of being a father, and now he is about to have three kids all under the age of three! And to think, he thought *I* was brave.

The training régime H and Cat prepared was brilliant. For instance when they realised one of my opponents — the Mexican brawler Kirino Garcia — had a tendency to wrestle on the ropes they were concerned it could make my legs weary. They arranged three of the Eels biggest men Fuifui, Feleti and Aaron Cannings to wrestle with me for 30 second periods in between my footwork training. That involved racing through 'ladders' to help me maintain quick feet. It was exhausting, but I loved it. I also enjoyed weights with them because I realised as I heaved great amounts of metal in short, sharp bursts to develop my explosive power, my 'mirror muscles' were replaced by genuine gain. Apart from increasing my explosiveness, my agility improved too. In the first year I trained under Hayden and Craig I gained such a strong foundation we only needed to 'tweak to peak' in the gym.

We always spoke about the thrill of winning a world title together, and it is great to think we realised our dream. However, I literally terrorised them at training and drove them nuts, constantly pulling pranks on them or worse still

I'd bite large chunks out of their already thinning hair when we wrestled. For Christmas I am buying them each a new watch, and they'll work better than the ones they have because their current watches seem to suggest I regularly turn up to appoinments late! Having them in my corner was a pleasure, and a great advantage. Indeed, it was almost an unfair advantage.

CHAPTER 37

DENTS IN THE STEEL SPINE

When former World Boxing Organization light-heavyweight champion Julio Gonzalez landed a wicked hook to my back during a willing sparring session outside Los Angeles, I thought a wrecking ball had crushed my internal organs. I've had my jaw broken, my hand smashed and my nose busted seven times through boxing, but no injury matched the pain I endured for the ensuing three weeks. The injury wouldn't allow me to do the simplest of things such as pick up Chloe, bend over to tie my shoelaces or enjoy uninterrupted sleep. I even had to stand up to watch a DVD or a fight tape. Two chiropractors, one in LA the other in Sydney, initially blamed the pain on severe bruising. However, an MRI scan eventually revealed Senor Gonzalez's right fist had shattered the L2 and L3 transverse process [the wings that come off your vertebrae] in my spine. While I know this will sound crazy to some people my reaction to the news was one of relief because I was concerned I might have become soft.

You see, so many people were adamant I'd suffered nothing more than deep bruising they'd dismiss my concern. Yet with each new day it was harder to train.

I sparred Gonzalez to fine-tune my skills before a world-title eliminator against the WBC's top contender Scott Pemberton, a Yankee brawler with a murderous punch. His other claim to fame was that he featured on the FBI's most wanted list because of allegations he was a standover man and debt collector for an alleged drug trafficker. While Pemberton denied the claims he accepted a plea bargain in 2002 and spent nine months in prison. 'I didn't extort no money from no one,' he said in an interview after his release. 'I went out and collected money from a kid for a so-called friend. I was a collector.'

As he marked time in prison reality bit Pemberton — and hard. It was reported the big hitter realised he'd not only cost himself a possible chance to fight for the world title but he'd also lost many decent pay days. When we agreed to fight in Perth his agent gave me a huge confidence boost when he requested the loser be paid a $US50,000 'compensation' fee because of the negative impact defeat would have on the beaten man's career. It was a joke, and I refused to entertain the idea. While his suggestion was hardly the talk of a man backing his charger's ability I still headed to America for quality sparring to enhance my chances.

It seemed a blessing to hook up with Gonzales because he was preparing to fight England's IBF champion Clinton Woods. Our first session was hard and fast. I felt as if I was in control but disaster struck. I remember the lead-up to my injury as Gonzalez doubled up on the jab and followed with a right hook to my head. I'd read the play and when he double-jabbed a second time I covered my head with my left hand and pivoted my torso to my right. That exposed the lower left side of my torso but I did that to 'ride' his punch. It's a method to help defuse some of the power in an opponent's shot. However, instead of slamming home the anticipated hook to my head Gonzalez went downstairs and crushed a right hook to my back. My spine was only exposed for a split second but he didn't miss.

The aftershock from the blow was an excruciating pain that speared straight down my left butt cheek, and when it settled just above my left thigh I could quite easily have fallen to the ground. I hobbled for the rest of that round, but I guess the adrenaline helped mask the full extent of the problem because I was able to box on. In the first break between rounds I told my assistant coach David Birchell it felt as if my kidneys or nerves had been damaged. I finished two more rounds and hopped out. The sense of satisfaction I experienced from out-boxing Gonzalez quickly subsided when my body cooled down. I felt every bloody bump on the road during our 80-minute trip back to Hollywood. It felt as if I had a broadsword buried in the base of my back. I was hurting and needed help. We eventually tracked down a chiropractor and after he examined the source of my pain he decided it would be unwise to adjust it. Thank God he didn't. The chiropractor's initial thought was that it could be nothing more than a case of severe bruising and a displaced rib so he advised me to apply ice to it and to rest.

Rest, however, was out of the question. I was so focused

on fighting Pemberton to guarantee a third shot at Markus Beyer that I blocked the pain out of my mind and returned to the gym the following day to again tango with Gonzalez. While I moved more like the Tin Man from the *Wizard of Oz* than a world-ranked fighter I managed to mix it until the end of the fourth round of our scheduled six rounds. But then the pain forced me to quit. While I was cranky with myself for having to give up it made me appreciate that I was dealing with something far more serious than bruising.

We flew back to Australia and one of the first things I did was to arrange an X-ray. It showed nothing so I threw myself into heavy training under the guidance of my strength and conditioning team, Hayden Knowles and Craig Catterick. I ran gut-busting five-minute time trials, punishing sprint sessions, heaved weights and, of course, I boxed. It amazes me to think that at that time I came close to breaking the Parramatta Eels rugby league club's record for the five-minute time trial. I broke it on my second go after I recovered and wear that as a badge of honour. Each activity, however, seemed to create a new level of pain so I arranged for a savage massage to try and knead whatever the problem was out of my back. Can you believe it? I reckon at least a hundred tubes of *Painaway* cream were rubbed into my back to try and alleviate the problem. By that time I had started standing up to watch television because it was impossible to sit or even lie down.

My fight with Pemberton fell through two weeks later when an MRI revealed I'd suffered two serious fractures in my spine I felt relieved because we could treat the problem. I had to rest and recuperate, and plan what to do next. At least I wasn't soft.

CHAPTER 38

LIFE'S MILLION TO ONE SHOT

Every fighter has his own reason for boxing. Some, like me, do it because they are on a quest to win the world title; others do it to prove something, be it to themselves or their mates; a few box to pay the rent or to put food on the table for their family; and then there are the blokes who punch on because it is the only thing they know how to do. I faced a 36-year-old Mexican fighter named Kirino Garcia at Perth's Challenge Stadium in 2005 who stepped into the ring for each of those reasons — and perhaps more. While he was Mexico's reigning light-heavyweight champion the night we locked horns, Garcia was heckled by the spectators in the crowd who said he'd looked as if he'd scoffed one or two too many tacos in-between training sessions. Sledging, heckling, abuse — whatever you might call it — is something all athletes must deal with, whether we like it or not. Myself, I usually laugh it off. That truth is the guys who sledged Kirino that night would have shown respect if they knew what a true warrior he really was. I also wonder how quickly their hearts would have shrunk if confronted by Kirino in person.

As a youth in the Mexican border town of Ciudad Juarez hunger and poverty forced Kirino to become a petty thief, a gang member and a street hustler. More often than not he finished the day hungry or nursing fresh wounds courtesy of yet another street fight. His home was a cardboard shanty where he was at the mercy of a cruel alcoholic father who'd need no reason to belt him. By the time he'd turned 22 Kirino's body was covered in a series of scars and tattoos. He needed to get out. So the 'coyotes' — people smugglers — convinced him in 1990 he could escape his lot by fighting in the United States. To do that, however, he had to illegally enter the country, swimming across the Rio Grande — a great effort by a non-swimmer — and trudging for four hours into the Arizona desert to rendezvous with more coyotes who drove him to a fight hall in Tucson. He was paid a lousy $85 to let a junior middleweight pound him for three painful rounds. Kirino, who hadn't eaten anything solid in the two days before the bout, said the hiding was well worth the meal the money allowed him to buy.

That was his lot for four long years. In that time he fought 18 bouts for no wins and he gained no perks for his trade. While most fighters are put up in hotels, fed and transported around the city they are fighting in, Kirino slept in doorways and back alleys while he waited for his fights and he could only eat after he was paid. He was trapped in a vicious cycle and learning about his struggle made me appreciate how lucky we fighters in Australia are. Very few of us *have* to fight; we do have other options in life and I think any boxer — or anyone for that matter — who thinks they're doing it tough in the Lucky Country should take note of Kirino's story because it should make them count their blessings.

Kirino's life changed when he was picked up the manager Olvaldo Kuchle and made to train hard in the gym. Kirino had believed because he was a street fighter he didn't need to train, but with fitness — and greater finesse — the victories soon stacked up. He fought ten former world champions and beat five of them. The night I fought him in Perth I found him to be a tough and dangerous puncher. His fearless attitude and stamina was thoroughly appreciated by me, the 5000-strong crowd and the hundreds of thousands of TV viewers. He never took a backward step and through a gutsy display he proved his worth as Mexico's national light-heavyweight champion. While he might have appeared unfit, Garcia had a rock-hard head that I reckon could withstand a dynamite blast! He had the ability to absorb some wicked body shots. I *know* I hurt him a few times, I could see it in his eyes but as a veteran of 67 fights he had far too much pride to give in and I respected his struggle. The Challenge Stadium bout was the second under my new trainer, Ismael Salas, and I wanted to get some rounds under my belt to try a few new moves we'd worked on at training — like boxing off the back foot. Garcia's determination to stand and deliver allowed me the opportunity to do that. I was aware he had a reputation to whack so I was careful not to engage in a toe-to-toe duel with him. I found I enjoyed boxing off the back foot and employing movement and angles to defuse his onslaught. For a change *I* was the matador and I was pitted against a genuine Mexican bull. At the end of the tenth and final round, each of the three judges declared me the unanimous winner [they each scored the fight 100-90] but Garcia won my wholehearted respect.

Garcia is one of the heart-warming stories in boxing, a sport often maligned for its blood thirstiness and mercenary characters. In fact, the fight game has been a blessing for Kirino, a father of two. He now owns a house and is considered to be well off by Mexican standards. While the fight game may not have quite taken him from the gutter to greatness, it has allowed him to enjoy a life that once seemed beyond reach.

CHAPTER 39

MUNDINE MADNESS

For five long years Australians had been spoiling for Anthony Mundine and me to fight, so it was no surprise that our weigh-in at Aussie Stadium was, in a word, wild.

The fight was secured after a series of negotiations between my camp and Mundine's manager Khoder Nasser that seemed to take forever. Both parties were happy with the deal and both parties kept their word — a rare occurrence in the fight game. The media had dubbed it a 'super bout' and it seemed as if all of Sydney turned out to watch the pair of us stand on the scales. Television camera crews, photographers, reporters and supporters from both corners jostled for prime position. I'm sure Channel Nine's veteran sports presenter Ken Sutcliffe would testify that it was every man for himself because he was unable to get to the scales for his live report to *A Current Affair* because no-one would sacrifice their place for him. I won't forget the madness in a hurry. Mundine's supporters screamed at me; my supporters dished it out to him. Journalists yelled out questions I had no hope of deciphering above the din, and from my vantage point the crowd seemed 20 deep.

The scene made a bigger impression on me later on than it did at the time because I was in an intense zone then. I was focused on the fight and I was trying to keep a few demons at bay — the cruellest of the lot being the death of my beautiful little niece, Brendan's daughter Sophie.

Out of respect for Brendan and his wife Julia's privacy I won't go into the details of the tragedy except to say that she went to sleep and didn't wake up. Her passing had a devastating impact on my entire family and the wounds will never heal. Mere words will never describe the grief and shocking pain my brother and his family have been through, and will endure in the future. It was the darkest time of my life, and there was no way I could fight in that mental state. Rather than allow Sophie's death to become a news story, I used a back injury as my excuse to put the fight back a month. I'd suffered a few spasms during training, but I could have pushed through it. But the pain in my heart made it impossible for me to box. I didn't like pulling the rug out from under Mundine because I know only too well the frustration of being in full training only to have an opponent suffer an injury or fall sick. It prolongs the dieting, the training and the mental build-up. While Mundine's camp weren't officially informed of the real reason I needed to delay the fight, I suspect Khoder Nasser was aware of what had happened. It's to his credit that when Nasser learnt I couldn't fight he didn't put on a song and dance. He simply said we'd find an alternative date. His shrug of the shoulder acceptance was a gesture not lost on me. We agreed to put the bout back a month, and while I thought that might have been time enough to galvanize my heart and soul I found out the hard way it definitely wasn't. Sadly, I don't think a lifetime will be.

There were other problems. The battle to make weight had sapped the spark out of me and I also 'peaked' a fortnight too early. It was not a good preparation, but as I stood on those scales and embraced the emotion of the crowd I believed I would be victorious. I had faith in my inner mongrel to shut everything out. When Sutcliffe finally fought his way through the throng to report live to the studio he asked me a question but I had bugger all to say. I simply gave the V for victory sign and went out to a back room and slugged down two Powerades, ate a few bananas and some bread. I then headed to the Splash Restaurant in King Street where Sav and the gang served a king-sized feast of pasta.

An hour or so before the weigh-in I'd laughed myself silly during the car trip after Bowdo noticed the 'look' I'd adopted for the fight. You see, during one of the idle moments during training and resting I grabbed a set of clippers and gave myself a mohawk. I did it to amuse myself, and I laughed even louder when David Birchell accepted my dare to follow suit because it did him no favours. As well as my Mohawk I also wore an army-style camouflage jacket that was in vogue at the time. As we drove towards Aussie Stadium a pair of monster hands slammed down on my shoulders from behind and Bowdo's voice boomed 'I've got it' so loudly I actually jumped. He pointed out that I looked like Travis Bickel, Robert De Niro's character in the movie *Taxi Driver*. For a split second my blood ran cold because I thought to myself, 'He's right.' However rather than worry about it I joined in the laughter and did my best imitation of De Niro's most memorable line. 'Are you talkin' to me?'

Bowdo's observation helped release a lot of the tension that had built up. I was concerned because I peaked two weeks before the bout. It happened as I sparred 12 rounds in a physically intense session, and it was as much a psychological blow as a physical one. I hadn't intended on being so intense during that session but after 12 rounds I wouldn't have blown out a candle. Salas and Birchy looked at me stunned. They were spinning out at how full-on I sparred. I didn't realise it, but I'd really stepped up the intensity. I belted my American sparring partner so badly in our seven rounds we'd had to send him back to the States the following day. He was cut and badly beaten and my other partner copped it hard for the remaining five rounds. Incredibly, I only grew stronger as the session went on. Mentally, I was so driven to be at optimum physical condition I made the mistake of being too eager, and I peaked. The adrenaline that coursed through my body that night made it impossible for me to switch off and go to sleep until 3am. I tried to ignore the fact that I'd hit my peak early, but I became concerned when I started to tire way too early in the ensuing gym sessions. I have never trained harder for a fight in my life. The sessions were exhausting and pushed my body and mind to the absolute limit.

During the lead-up to the fight, I would walk into the gym with a poker face on and get straight to work. There wasn't my usual piss-taking or practical jokes. It was all business. I now think torturing myself was some sort of subconscious therapy to try and rid me of the pain I felt about my niece. I figured flogging myself in the gym would take my mind off that agony. The whole lead-up to the fight was a blur. My thoughts concentrated on my brother, Julia, their boys Tom and Lewis and, of course, Sophie. While I appreciate the fight was considered history in the making, I could not escape the fact that my family — which is my life — was hurting badly. I tried to conserve energy in those final two weeks, but it was hard because my appetite was insane. I had to train hard to burn the kilojoules.

The Mundine bout confirmed it was time for me to move up a weight division because the dieting and training took too tough a toll on my body. I had dieted for five long months; trained like a Spartan in late-night sparring sessions at Billy Sparsis's Padded Gloves gym at Glebe; ate my dinner late at night because I wanted to prepare myself to fight at that time. My body-fat levels worried a couple of doctors. They were down to 3 per cent, and the fact that an elite athlete carries 10 per cent should emphasise how low mine was. My fat level was measured by a computer-programmed X-ray worth $250,000 and the doctor who monitored it said under normal circumstances a person with so low a reading would be hospitalised because of the risks to their health. My body was starving so I could make the weight limit, but my doctor monitored me closely just in case I went into meltdown. To help melt any fat I may have accumulated during the day I'd also sit in bathwater so hot that I'd recoil even when I stuck my finger into it. The water would have been hot enough to boil a lobster but I had to do it because I needed to burn up the food I had consumed that day so I could have breakfast the next morning to give me fuel for that day's training. I'd just cup the family jewels and plunge into the cauldron. It wasn't the healthiest of practices but I had no choice. It was the only way I could make the super-middleweight limit. I was going through physical and mental torture.

According to the newspapers Mundine had his own problems, namely a tearful split with his father-trainer, Tony. I took no notice, let alone any comfort, from the reports because I guessed Mundine was using some of his mates in the media to lull me into a false sense of confidence. I refused to allow that to happen. Indeed, that was one of the few things I had control over.

There were other aspects of the build-up I found very hard to stomach. While Mundine and I didn't see each other at either of our two press conferences it angered me to learn he had used his time in front of the microphones and cameras to try and turn the fight into something much more than a match between two men: he played the race and religion cards and I didn't like it. I didn't appreciate it because in the climate we were in (and still are) he was meddling with fire. He said I represented white corporate Australia while he was fighting for the oppressed. I don't know where that view came from but I was quick to point out that my roots were blue-collar working class. I'm a humble carpenter. The press conference was an exercise in pettiness. I was told I was not to walk on the red carpet he had laid out from the dressing room to the halfway mark of the football field. It was a few hundred metres in length and I'm reliably told he strutted every step of the way in a suit that was described in the *Sydney Morning Herald* as a 'gangsta get-up'.

For reasons I have never bothered to explore, Mundine insisted on fronting the press first. It was the same when we fought our double-header in Perth in December 2005. Then he all but threatened to hold his breath until he turned blue unless he was the main event. As Mundine had made it clear I was not to tread on his red carpet, so Bowdo arranged for a stretch limousine to drive me onto the field. It trumped Mundine's tired old red carpet entrance.

The questions I was asked were based on what Mundine had said and it was predictable hot air. I refused to bite. Regardless of my annoyance at his attempt to turn it into a race war I shook hands with his father Tony after the presser wrapped up. I appreciated the fact there was a sense of mutual respect. I loved watching him fight on old TV ringside tapes and respected him for having been a hell of a fighter.

A lot of people said I would murder Mundine. They thought he'd crumble under the weight of my heavier punches and while I obviously valued such support, I didn't allow it to lull me into a false sense of security. A false state of confidence has been responsible for bringing more fighters undone than anything else. I was ringside when Mundine fought the Great Dane Mikell Kessler for his WBA belt at the Sydney Entertainment Centre, and while Mundine lost what struck me most about my arch rival was the improvement in his overall game plan — the most notable aspect being his confidence. I was braced for a tough bout, a genuine challenge, but a victory all the same.

CHAPTER 40

FRIGHT NIGHT

I'm sitting inside the dressing room at Aussie Stadium in the countdown to what is being called the biggest fight in Australian boxing history. I can hear the crowd screaming and shouting during the preliminary bouts. They're whipping themselves up for the main event — the Man versus the Machine. I'm amazed that, despite the hype, I don't feel the slightest hint of nerves. The adrenaline is smashing through my body like a tsunami, but the butterflies that come to life in my gut before my big fights are nowhere to be found. I'm pumped! I want to get it on now. I've waited five long years for this moment; five years of being called a 'bum' and a 'nothing' by a footballer.

In the lead-up the 'experts' predict the loser's career will be over but I don't agree. They're merely highlighting their ignorance. Foreman wasn't finished when Ali iced him. Sugar Ray Leonard was still a hot commodity after he lost to Roberto Duran. There'll still be big fights for Mundine —

world titles included — when I've finished with him. Well so I think. I haven't even considered the idea of being defeated. Whenever I've thought about our showdown it's always ended in Mundine being badly busted up and bloodied. Yet, I'm not cocky. I'm not stupid enough to listen to those people who are adamant it'll be a walkover. Every second punter seems to have put money on me to knock him out. I appreciate their faith, but I know Mundine is a serious challenge; he's a threat. I have good hands, but his are quicker than mine. I'm physically stronger, but Mundine has played first-grade rugby league and anyone who has watched that code knows you must be strong to play it. I punch harder than he does — I know that — but he has a hard punch too. It's a great match-up and it's anyone's fight.

Sophie's photo is taped to my glove. Tears stream down Brendan's and my faces. I think I can subdue the uselessness I'm feeling about her passing by 'taking' her out there with me. It's my attempt to shine some light but it is tough.

The call comes for me to enter the ring first. I hug the people in the dressing room. If they're not family, they're close enough to it. I kiss my brother on the cheek. He knows who this fight is for. Heavy emotion fills the air. I feel not one ounce of nerves, just a steely and overwhelming sense of determination to fulfill my tribute. This is it. Judgement day. There's no turning back, not that I want to. I'm prepared to take on 100 men and not bat an eyelid.

The walk to the ring is very intense. Depending on which corner they're in people scream words of support or yell abuse. I recognise no-one because the walk is a blur. The intensity of the mood at the stadium hits me like a shovel in the face. Still, no nerves. This is crazy. Where are the butterflies? Then it happens. I look at my brother Brendan and I feel all the pain he has felt, the pain we've shared is ugly and brutal. I actually want to cry because I can still see his sadness; it's cloaked around him and suffocates us all. He is as hard as nails. BG doesn't want to show anything, doesn't want his brother to lose this fight. Any fight for that matter. My heart is heavy at seeing him, and I find it hard to focus. I am, however, brimming with pride at the honourable way in which he has conducted himself after such a devastating loss. There are 30,000 screaming people frothing at the mouth while millions are watching it on television across the nation. Yet, my focus is on my brother's hurt and the loss of his beautiful daughter. My desire to be in the centre of the ring is broken and I fight to get my head back where it needs to be. I climb through the ropes and get the feel of the ring. I see the mass of people, all staring, all yelling. They want blood. Most seem to want Mundine's head on a platter. I am thinking more about Sophie than anything else, yet I plan to grant them their wish. However, the emotion I'd experienced since Sophie's passing meant my focus shifted from beating Mundine, to winning for my family and winning for my niece. A big mistake but it proved I'm only human.

Mundine announces his arrival with hip hop crap. 'Here we go,' I think to myself. The 'Showman'. I can see the flags his entourage are carrying, but they don't seem to be in any rush to get into the ring. He's soaking it up like some kind of royal. It strikes me as funny that, when he enters the ring, after five long years of badgering and taunting one another this is the closest we've ever been to each other. Now we're 5 metres apart and ready to rumble. As I move around the ropes I look at the people peering at us. I see faces that belong to the who's who of Australian society: people from the media, show business, sport and the underworld. The ones I look for though are my family, friends and supporters. I'll never forget the look on the face of Julia, Brendan's wife, Sophie's mum. I caught sight of her blank grief and tear-filled eyes. I just wanted to leave the ring and embrace her. I had to concentrate to restrain my tears. It's the closest my legs came to buckling all night. I look at Brendan as the referee lays down the law and we're told to come out fighting. Funny, I didn't think either of us would need to be told to do that.

I open up in the first round. I'm smashing him. There's no hate in my punches, though, I know people might not believe that. I just want to beat him. I've won the first round through aggression, but I'm cooked. In three frenzied minutes I've spent all my energy. I'm not surprised. The weeks and months building up to this moment have taken a massive toll on my body as I've had to do all sorts of severe things to make the super-middleweight limit. The tank is empty after just one round. Eleven more to go. But I can dig deep. The pink band on my left arm to honour Sophie will give me the strength I so desperately need.

I'm over-anxious to hit Mundine, so I'm telegraphing my blows. He can see them coming and evades them easily.

'Stay in close, mate. Difficult for him to hit there.'

The rounds go quickly, but I don't feel as if I'm in the fight. Sophie is on my mind and I feel as if I'm on top of the light tower 20 metres above the ring looking down on the battle, and I don't like what I see. I'm behind on points, but I'm trying so bloody hard. The zip just isn't there. Mundine's punches don't stop coming. I make a mistake, I drop my hands after I almost slip in a puddle of water and he launches himself at me — an uppercut and left hook. They're crisp shots and they land clean on my chin.

'*Would I have done that?*'

It doesn't matter. Shots that would KO most fighters had no impact on me.

'*So, is that the best you've got?*'

Still, he's winning and I have to find a knockout punch. Where the hell is it? I'm throwing them, but my strength and my energy have long gone. My big punch is in the puddles of sweat that dot the canvas. I feel like the captain of a ship that's sinking, but I'll be stuffed if he's going to knock me down. I'll die before that. Sounds ridiculous, I know, but they way I'm feeling I'm prepared to die. I'm now fighting just to finish on my feet. The script wasn't meant to be like this.

The twelfth and final round. Mundine and I embrace. It's a sign of mutual respect. He's been a good opponent, the better fighter on the night. However, I can still win by knockout. Most men would have wilted by now, so I step it up a notch. I try … *and I try* … but it's not there. I've left nothing in the tank. The fight ends. I know I've lost. I congratulate Mundine for his performance. He is a worthy winner and I have no excuses. He tells me all the stuff that has been said in the build-up to this night was never personal. I finish his sentence by saying, 'I know, it was only ever business'. The judges reward him. Michael Lee gives him the fight 116-113. Pinij Prayadsab scores it 118-111 and Derek Milham 118-112. He's won by a unanimous decision.

Mundine has the microphone and I wait to hear him skite, to say 'I told you so.' But those words don't leave his lips, and I'm surprised. Instead he acknowledges what he calls a good fight. While I am in hell I think highly of him for being gracious in victory. I extend the courtesy. I tell Australia that Mundine deserved the victory, that he was the better fighter on the night. I tell the mob I'll be back and leave for the dressing room where I'm overwhelmed by a surge of emotion. My friends and family bleed for me and try to console me with hugs. I am beaten, but I realise boxing is a sport where the man who doesn't turn up to fight on the night will lose. Mundine turned up to Aussie Stadium on 17 May 2006 with his game on. I didn't. I can live with that, but others can't.

The media and 'boxing experts' are into me in the immediate aftermath of the fight, saying I should retire. I can't believe what I'm hearing. Retire? Did they say that about West Coast when they lost the 2005 grand final? Did they say because they lost to Sydney they should stand down from the competition? No. Boxing in Australia is different: a fighter gets beaten and they say it's all over. I don't understand that mentality. It was only the second defeat of my career. In the first bout against Beyer I was disqualified after I flogged him for five rounds. I lost a close rematch to him and it wasn't a terrible loss. And now Mundine. Retire?

What do they know? I am the fighter and that decision is up to me. I bury my head into a towel and cry my heart out. The defeat has nothing to do with my tears. I can cop any sporting loss on the chin fair and square. I cry instead for Sophie. I cry for Brendan, Julia and my two nephews. I cry for the injustice of it all.

I return to my hotel to be with my crew and drink cups of tea, not beer. I absorbed a bit of punishment and the last thing my body needs is alcohol. The disappointment of defeat is sinking in. I'm gutted and I wonder if life can be the same again? Selfish thought. Of course it can. My family has just experienced a terrible tragedy. However, I am depressed. My mates stand beside me. God knows a man is lucky to have such friends.

I try to sleep. Impossible. I keep thinking about the fight, about not being able to get going when it mattered. I'm tormented all night by the fact that he had the tactics and I fought 11 rounds without energy. The next morning I drive the 40-minute trip to pick Chloe up from Arie Plug's house, and the radio is buzzing with reports of the fight. It was as if the news readers were trying to remind me of my loss. There's no escaping it. The newspaper headlines with the loss in big, black, bold print. Chloe, however, is my salvation. She gives me a hug. She doesn't care about the fight. She has better things to talk about — the Wiggles, dogs and cats — and I love it. All seems good in the world, and I hug her as if I'll never let her go.

The memory of the fight returns. Where did it go wrong? I wonder if I paid him too much respect in the build-up.

Maybe I talked up his chances in my mind way too much. My build-up was way too intense: I barred media from watching me spar; I blacked out windows so people couldn't spy on me at the gym; I didn't talk at the press conferences. It wasn't me. I like to joke and have fun and I promise to follow that path in the future.

I front to a press conference on the roof of my hotel. They want me to remove my sunglasses, which are hiding the punishment I took, so they're not leaving my head. The press want to know if I'm going to hang up the gloves. They obviously didn't listen to me in the ring because I made it clear I'd be back, so I keep 'em guessing. I tell them I'm taking some time out to chill. Most shake my hand and wish me well — no matter what I decide.

SOPHIE

Having my own precious daughter, the most adorable little thing, I knew how much sunshine to your days, your litte princess was going to bring.
I was in Sydney training, before I laid eyes on your little girl.
And just as I expected, she had your hearts in a whirl.
I looked in the pram at you, Sophie, and heard your dad say, 'You wanna hold?'
I looked at him as if to say, 'Whaddayou reckon?'. I didn't need to be told!
I picked you up and smelt that smell only a baby can own,
It had been one minute, I was clucky already, you had me completely thrown.
Your tiny hands, your tiny nails, that little face so cute,
You were sweeter than a box of Fruit Loops, the ones that go 'crunch to boot'.
You captivated everyone, with your eyes so alive and blue.
There was no mistaking where you came from, you were a Stevens/Green through and through.
You were such a gorgeous angel, but goodness knows you didn't like to sleep,
It took hours of cradling and caressing, and finally off Mum and Dad would creep.
You melted the heart of your tough old Dad, you made him so content and proud,
He was just so in love with you, Soph, he wanted to shout it out loud.
That night on the kitchen table, you cast a spell and were holding court,
Who was to know your blossoming life was to be so cruelly cut short.

Time stood still, hearts caved in, rivers were cried, lives shook,
Whoever has bloody taken you doesn't realise how much they took.
I felt sick I wasn't able to soak up your family's anger and strain,
Just wanted to king hit that horrific feeling that was dishing out the pain.
You'd be so proud of your daddy, Sophie, granite strength etched across his hurting face,
I was honoured to be standing across from him, lowering you to your final resting place.
Your parents have showed some hope and guts, which is something to admire,
Just getting out of bed some days must take some inner fire.
Your two big brothers miss like heck their beautiful little sis,
But the one thing they have forever is the memory of your kiss.
Amazingly another addition has come into your family's life,
A little gem called Mia Sophie, who's sure to get into a bit of strife.
Don't ever worry, little princess, I'll always look out for those you love,
We all know you're out there, flying around like a peaceful white dove.
I talk to you like you're with us, 'cause you will always be one of our clan,
Just like your Uncle Mike said, I'm proud to be your Uncle Dan.

SOPHIE JOSEPHINE GREEN
3/11/2005 — 8/3/2006

CHAPTER 41

A VERY PRIVATE PAIN

Four weeks after losing to Anthony Mundine I was bed ridden in a Perth hospital with an ailment some of the state's best medical minds diagnosed as a 'mystery illness'. Pain hammered my body and left me slumped in a heap. When I was asked to describe the nature of my pain I'd tell them it felt as if I'd been gutted by a knife and stitched back up with barbed wire. I wasn't exaggerating. I was in hospital for eight agonising days post-Mundine and apart from having a tube stuck up my backside, down my throat and nose, I was also subjected to just about every medical test imaginable. At one point I was placed on a morphine drip for five days to help make my life more bearable.

In the 30 months leading into the Mundine bout I was hospitalised on five occasions due to what I'll call 'pain episodes'. It was something I chose to keep secret from everyone except those closest to me, mainly because the medical fraternity couldn't identify the problem. I was especially reluctant to let the media know about my predicament after the Mundine loss because I didn't want anyone to interpret it as an excuse. (I have said on numerous occasions Mundine was the better fighter on that particular night, and I'll maintain that until the day I die.) The attacks normally lasted a fortnight but what added to my frustration was the numerous scans and X-rays I underwent that revealed nothing. There were times, I assure you, when I lay in that hospital bed fearing the worst. That experience has made empathise so much with people, especially kids, who suffer from serious illnesses.

The first time I suffered an attack was two weeks after the Sean Sullivan fight when my brain basically stewed in its own juices. I was eventually advised to see a specialist who was described as 'a little bit alternative'. By this stage, post Mundine the problem had reached a critical point, and I couldn't have cared less if he was a witch doctor from the Congo. I just needed a cure. From our first meeting I was convinced he could help me. He looked at the file crammed with numerous reports and dismissed them as 'fucking useless', a 'fucking waste of time' and quickly established I was not only lactose intolerant but also suffered from a rare pancreas problem. An enzyme that should have been discharged from my pancreas while I ate was dormant, and the consequence of that was a sugar overload in my system. The doctor engineered a massive overhaul of my diet which eliminated almost all sugar and dairy. I must admit that didn't particularly appeal to me, I lived on Redskins lollies in my early days, and my new eating regime meant zero tolerance approach to sweets. I've since discovered some great tasting dishes including barbecued seafood and meat, some vegetables (fruit and vegetables have to be carefully monitored because they contain sucrose and fructose, a form of sugar) while I go mad in coffee shops with weak soy lattes. Occasionally I'll eat foods and consume beverages (like beer) that I should steer well clear of. I suffer for my foolishness when I indulge because my body gives me a sharp reminder — a literal painful kick in the guts — to ensure I pull my head in and stay on the straight and narrow.

CHAPTER 42

BUSH BASHED

Perhaps it was the woman who damned me for letting her down by losing to Anthony Mundine. Or maybe it was the bloke with a heavyweight beer gut who philosophised that there was nothing worse in the world than being a loser that helped me realise I needed to go bush to escape the attention I received after my high-profile defeat.

I was genuinely floored by the number of people who went out of their way to console me after my loss but it was frustrating to be told by dozens of other people how I should have fought Mundine. I believe I handled the defeat with dignity. While losing was very hard to take, thinking of the crosses people around the world have to bear — such as illness, conflict, poverty and death put my sense of 'grief' into perspective.

Apart from thinking of people in a worse boat than me I also took comfort in history and thinking about how the holy trinity of heavyweights — Muhammad Ali, Joe Frazier and

George Foreman — were among a long list of great fighters who climbed off the canvas to reach boxing's greatest heights. Yet it was clear I needed time out from the world. I needed to escape the seemingly endless attention. After eight weeks — punctuated by a painful stint in Perth's main hospital — I reached the stage where I just didn't want to talk about the fight anymore. It wasn't that I couldn't handle the defeat, it was quite the opposite actually. I watched a replay of the fight not long after that night in Sydney and while it stung me to relive it I had to do it in order to move on with my career. After I hit the stop button on the DVD's remote control I tipped my hat to Mundine for a job well done, absorbed all the hurt and disappointment and held my head high.

A few weeks on the road with Brendan and Benny O'Donnell seemed a brilliant idea. We loaded up BG's car and hit the road for a trip that made the early explorers Burke and Wills, who perished in 1861 during their attempt to cross the continent from north to south, seem like a well-organised walk in the park. Funnily enough the trip where anything that could possibly go wrong went horribly wrong was the perfect remedy for my soul.

We left Perth at 10pm and while our mission was to simply follow the coast north we somehow took a wrong turn and ended up inland, in the middle of nowhere. We just shrugged our shoulders. I remember our seafood feast under the stars as one of the best meals I've enjoyed. We had car problems, and BG and I left out camp to get it repaired. We hired another 4WD. We were gone for hours and on our return we were 'greeted' by the sight of Benny doing star jumps —

completely starkers. He offered no explanation; we asked for none. On our way to our camp site we clipped five kangaroos and the trailer's wheel arch was left stuffed after one of the collisions. Five hundred metres from our destination we became bogged in sand — trailer and all. Somehow we managed to laugh about it. Forty eight hours after we left home — and 33 hours behind schedule — we finally set up camp in the dark.

The next morning I unzipped my tent and was greeted by paradise. We were 20 metres from shore and I enjoyed an unblemished view of long waves firing off down the line on the outer relief. Peace at last.

Nonetheless, the dramas continued. During our 12-day escapade the car battery went flat; the generator constantly broke down; the wind blew our tent over a couple of times; the jet ski conked out in treacherous surf a kilometre off shore; the dinghy's outboard motor packed it in; Benny needed stitches after he slashed his foot; we became bogged five times; a swarm of mice raided our supplies; the wind blew sand into every meal; and our surfboards flew off the roof of our car as we motored down the highway at 120 kilometres an hour. We were so weary when we tied them back onto the roof we didn't realise we'd tied the doors shut and couldn't get into the bloody car. We had to start all over again.

Then there was the tiger shark. I was at a location I choose to keep secret waiting for a wave when I first saw him — all 3.6 metres of him — and he was less than 3 metres from my board. I only became aware of the shark's presence when he rolled over on his side with a soft splash. I could see the big fella was munching on a turtle. He was so close to me before he sunk slowly beneath the surface that I swear I heard his teeth gnashing through the shell and flesh. It was so crazy a scene I turned to another surfer, who was a long-term local, and asked if he'd also seen the shark.

'Yeah, mate,' he said. 'He's always here having a feed. Don't worry about him, he's alright.'

It took a few seconds for his answer to register but when I looked at the bloke I could see he was in his late 40s so I guessed it was safe to presume he'd survived over a long period of time without incident.

While I continued surfing on some beautiful waves I kept one wary eye out for my friend with the big dorsal fin. I was out in that tiger shark's hunting ground for two hours, and when Brendan and Benny eventually joined me I kept quiet about the 'Noah' because, after realising he had no interest in eating humans, I didn't want to cause them unnecessary concern. Funnily enough they didn't seem to appreciate my thoughtfulness when I told them about the shark back on shore.

Our trip worked wonders for me. After my stint in hospital and the Mundine result it helped to know I could still laugh at the same dumb things I had laughed at before that night at Aussie Stadium. I could still appreciate majestic sunsets. I could still enjoy time with people I cared for. And I could surf beside a tiger shark, too! One of my most memorable trips ever with the perfect company.

CHAPTER 43

SOPHIE DELEZIO

As much as I was in pain after the Mundine fight, it was nothing compared to the lot of little Sophie Delezio. I was at Sophie's bedside when this little champion of champions showed signs she would recover from the second accident that required for her to be placed on a life support machine, and I could've cried like a baby. I was in the ward at the invitation of her father Ron, a man whose inner strength and capacity for acceptance never ceases to amaze me. Sophie captured all Australians' hearts in 2003 when she suffered burns to 85 per cent of her body after a car ploughed into a day-care centre in the Sydney suburb of Fairlight during the kids' nap time. Despite countless prayers and positive thoughts from millions of people, doctors needed to amputate her feet and some fingers in the weeks that followed. I listened to the reports and anecdotes relayed by people such as broadcaster Alan Jones and I admired what I heard about the girl's spirit and the family's strength. While she was only two at the time her tenacity and will to pull through such a shocking ordeal made a deep impression on me.

Ironically, a week before her second accident I had phoned Ron and asked if Sophie would do me the honour of carrying the Aussie flag into the ring for me before my bout with Mundine, because I couldn't think of a more worthy person. In my eyes she personified the best of the true Aussie character.

Then I received a phone call from Peter Kogoy, a journalist with *The Australian*, to ask if I'd heard what had happened to Sophie. I had no idea what he was talking about but when I heard the extent of her injuries I needed to sit down because I felt so gutted for her and the Delezio family. For the life of me I couldn't understand what that girl could possibly have done to deserve such a fate. At the time the only thing I could think to do was to take a teddy bear and some flowers to her. It didn't seem fair, and as I drove towards the hospital I remembered how I'd become acquainted with her family three years earlier in the aftermath of that first accident. I received a letter asking if I could donate some signed gloves to help raise funds to assist Sophie and the other little girl injured in the fire, Molly Wood. It was nothing and I was happy to help, but what floored me was the beautiful letter I received from Ron and Carolyn thanking me for what they called a 'wonderful gesture'. What wonderful, selfless people they were. I sent a card wishing Sophie a speedy recovery while Nina picked out a pretty dress we hoped might help make her feel happy.

I left the hospital that day feeling very empty but a few days later Ron asked me to visit again and Sophie was in even worse shape. She was naked, on her side and breathing with the help of a ventilator. I didn't know what to expect before I walked in but I guess the shock I felt must've shown because Ron snapped me back to reality when he asked Sophie to 'Say hello to Danny'. Even though she wasn't in a conscious state she raised her hand and smiled at me. 'Holy crap,' I thought. 'She smiled ... Sophie smiled.' Then Ron said, 'Sophie, smile if you know Danny is here' and when she did I could have cried. 'You little champion,' I thought. I then let her know everyone loved her and that we were all thinking of her. 'Everyone wants you to get better,' I said trying not to talk at a million miles an hour. 'Keep fighting darling, you're an absolute legend.'

As we all know, little Sophie did pull through and since then I've kept in touch with her and her family. Chloe even played with Sophie and a few of her friends before I flew to Melbourne to fight Paul Murdoch in early 2007. Before Chloe met Sophie I told her that she'd been burned in an accident and that she looked 'different'. But I told her that didn't matter because, as she would find out for herself, Sophie is a beautiful, *beautiful* girl. It was quite special for me to see the kids play happily together that afternoon.

It's my sincere belief Sophie Delezio is on this earth to do something special. I am not religious by any stretch of the imagination but I believe a greater power would not allow her to endure all she has for no reason. She has conquered challenges that would break most hearts and spirits. Whenever I'm asked to nominate my heroes its not athletes, instead it's people like Sophie, her parents, her brother

Mitchell, the medical personnel and army of other people who help care for her that come straight to my mind. I've said it before but I think the government should remove the Queen from the two-dollar coin and replace her with Sophie as a tribute to her courage. The only problem with that is such a coin would be too precious for anyone to part with. Little Sophie, sweetheart, you epitomise the true Aussie spirit. We love you.

CHAPTER 44

NEED FOR SPEED

Not long after I announced my retirement from boxing I received a phone call from a representative for Brett 'The Boss' Stevens, who owns one of Australia's top drag racing teams, inviting me to consider an offer to be a driver for one of his six second quarter mile/ 380 kilometre top door slammers. At the time of writing this I have to admit the lure of belting up in one of their high octane fuelled vehicles is very bloody tempting — the adrenalin rush that would provide would definitely cure my need for excitement. Though, I have a date on a V8 Supercar raceway as a result of my last televised 'boxing' bout against Channel Seven's Grant Denyer on *Sunrise*. It was part of Grant's challenge segment where he does things like bungee jump out of a helicopter. He's deadset crazy but I love his spark and the fact that the little fella has more front than a block of flats by doing the crazy stunts impresses me. I made sure I didn't inflict too much pain on Grant when we boxed, but I was sure to let him feel just a *tiny* amount of the punishment a fighter goes through, plus it made for great TV. Our 'bout' ended in a draw but Grant, who, like me, is a Ford man through and through, upped the ante when he challenged me to race him in a V8 car. While I've accepted, I'll definitely be the underdog on the grid because away from his job as a television host, Denyer is one of Australia's top up and coming racing drivers.

As a kid I loved the *Mad Max* car — the supercharged Ford XB Interceptor was the focus of my attention when I watched Mel Gibson play the part of an adrenaline-fuelled futuristic cop. As a kid I day dreamed of screaming around the streets in a souped-up XB like Mad Max , and that love affair was rekindled two years ago when I attended a drag meet with my mate Jeff McGlinn, and I laid eyes on a lovingly restored model. You would've had to have been blind not to see how much I loved the car — I was frothing! Jeff said he'd build me one and that it would look much better than the one that left me in a near hypnotic trance. I realised he was serious a few weeks later when he phoned to say he'd not only located an XB but it was in perfect condition to be restored.

Jeff is a former diesel mechanic so he knows a hell of a lot about cars and he scribbled down notes as I told him I was after a machine that looked super tough and hard; one that went like the clappers and sounded ridiculously loud and throaty ... the way a 'big block' should sound!

With that Jeff responded with a sharp 'right Dan' and he set about to do what he does best — make things happen. I wanted my dream car to reflect a traditional Aussie muscle car, lots of rubber, chrome, straight lines and a slick interior.

Eighteen months later I received a call to go to Jeff's house to take a look at the finished project. When I saw it roll out of his stable, well, it was very much a case of love at first sight. There was nothing about the car that didn't blow my mind ... the interior is a work of art, the exterior is a masterpiece. The old girl pulls seriously hard, and spits and thunders like nothing else ... I was speechless. All I could do was to give Jeff a hug that threatened to crush his ribs and to thank him a hundred times. The crew — especially, Jamie and Keith Bounsel, Nathan Rabe and Greg Simms had worked wonders. The car is a real headturner, with young and old happy to appreciate its beauty. When I told Jeff I was going to sleep in it, he may have thought I was joking but I'd never been so serious about anything in my entire life. It is one of my pride and joys.

CHAPTER 45

DAMO

Before I fought the highly rated American Otis Griffin in July 2007, I decided to take a leaf from some of the world's best athletes and to 'get selfish' — to make my fight against the North American Boxing Organization's reigning champion the centre of my existence. That mindset came about because I figured one of the biggest problems in my preparation for previous campaigns was I allowed myself to be too distracted by outside events. I wanted to be tunnel-visioned against Griffin because apart from expecting a tough fight, victory would entitle me to a shot at either Antonio Tarver's IBO belt or Clinton Woods's IBF title. Though, to think too much about the possibility of another world-title shot was a distraction in itself because I needed to simply focus on Griffin, a man with a growing reputation. Apart from being a former professional Grid Iron player, in 2005 he made a name for himself by winning Oscar De La Hoya's reality boxing show *The Next Great Champ*. So I decided to block everything out around me; to ignore the rest of the world and to become an island. I was to unfortunately learn that 'selfish' concept goes against who I am. That 'hard edge' — as the sports psychologists call it — I craved disintegrated very quickly when I received word Damian 'Damo' Scott, a 12-year-old cancer patient I'd befriended in Perth, was on his deathbed. The news hit me like a brick and as I hung up the phone after speaking to him I felt absolutely gutted.

Damo and I struck up our friendship in 2005 during one of my visits to the Princess Margaret Hospital for Children. Seeing those kids rips my insides to pieces every time I go there, but as someone who has been blessed with good health and sporting success I consider it my duty to make time to meet the kids. They're low-key events where I take some Green Machine merchandise along with big bags of lollies to distribute to the children and their families. On one particular visit a nurse from the cancer unit asked if I'd spend some time with a young fellow she said would love to meet me. And that was how I met Damo. He was bald because of his chemotherapy treatment, but jeepers creepers the kid had some spark about him. "Ow ya goin', Danny Green?" was how he greeted me. He was 10 going on 20, and the longer we spoke the more it felt as if I was talking to an old mate. Damo was not only pretty sharp but he also took the piss out of me, bagging the fact I drove a Ford because 'Holdens rule' in his world. He then put it on me to buy a butterfly trinket he'd made out of clay. 'I normally charge people two bucks for these, but you're rich "Greeny" … you're rich … you can buy it for five dollars!' he said. He'd won me, cheeky glint in his eye and all. While his mother Sharon sighed and told him to behave, I couldn't stop smiling. I *liked* this kid. 'Five bucks?' I replied. 'Mate, this is a good piece ... a really good piece ... I think you've been underselling yourself here. I'm going to give you ... 60 bucks ... and Damo, I want to see that price raised mate. I don't want to be the only person ripped off here.' Well, if ever a kid looked as if he had won the lottery it was Damo, as one by one he counted out the notes and coins. He couldn't believe his luck. His mother told me not to pay so much but, Sharon, I got it cheap. His butterfly is priceless.

When I left the ward I gave Sharon my number and told Damo to keep in touch when they returned home to Manjimup, a three-and-a-half hour drive into timber country south-west of Perth — and it didn't surprise me when he called to say g'day. I received text messages, emails and phone calls that kept me up to date with his progress. It was approaching my birthday in March 2007 when Damo returned to Princess Margaret Hospital. I'd arranged to meet him at a certain time but I was delayed at a meeting that dragged on and on. Had I known that Damo sat outside the hospital for an hour waiting for me to turn up I would have walked out of the meeting and rescheduled it for later; it hurts me now to picture the little bloke waiting and waiting for a Ford — of all things — to roll up, wondering if I'd forgotten him. When I finally rocked up Damo was wearing his Holden T-shirt (to stir me) and before presenting me with a gigantic birthday card he must've spent ages working on he declared, 'Ford sucks'. He'd cut some green cardboard into the shape of boxing gloves and in his best handwriting he'd written: 'From one fighter to another; DAMO SCOTT IN REMISSION 2007 PS Holden still rule! It was absolutely brilliant.

The Make-A-Wish people helped Damo fulfil his dream to visit Disneyland and he was beaming when I saw him off at the airport. I met his entire family and I could see where Damo's qualities came from. His father John, mum Sharon, two brothers, little sister and grandparents were all good natured, decent people. He was so excited about the big adventure none of us could stop grinning at his joy; it was innocent and it was beautiful. When I hugged him goodbye he told me what I expected to hear: 'Ford suck.' With a wave and smile he was off on his way to see Mickey and Minnie Mouse and my wish for him was that he had the best time a kid could ever have. A few days later I received a text message which said; 'Damo here. Anything you want me to get you while I'm away? Got Chloe a present.' The kid was all heart.

Damo was supposed to be ringside at my fight in May 2007 against Puerto Rico's former WBA champion Manny Siaca, but the fight was cancelled when Siaca fell ill. It was disappointing, but as Damo and I agreed there'd always be next time. Unfortunately, I received a phone call before 'next time' arrived. The cancer had returned and I was shattered to hear it didn't look good. I phoned Damian and it was heartbreaking. He was heavily sedated to help fight the pain that wracked him. He made grunting sounds for words when he spoke and, as I found out from his parents, the tumour on his brain was so bad it made one of his eyes bulge out of its socket while he also bled constantly from his nose. When I hung up I felt so hollow. I agonised about flying from Sydney to visit him, I had a busy few days pencilled in my diary. I had to spar, train, watch tapes of Griffin; talk tactics with Salas and get massaged. The selfish stuff that makes winners. I had far too much on — the fight; a possible world title shot; a training program; tactics to devise. I was in turmoil. *Yes*, the fight was important, but Damo? He was my little mate. How could I possibly let him down? I couldn't just block him out. My heart doesn't work like that. The need to be selfish was scrapped because the moment I thought about the bigger picture — a friend in need — I had to go. After I booked the first available flight to Perth I rang Nina to tell her my plan, but she wasn't surprised. Nina said she knew I'd fly back, even as I spoke about the 'reasons' that tied me to Sydney.

When I got to Manjimup, Damo was in palliative care and I saw the doctors had stuck a tube into his chest and that they'd also placed a patch over his eye. Yet, even in his terrible pain Damo's character shone through. He did his best to crack jokes when it sounded as though every word he spoke was tortured and he constantly smiled. Then, in an enormous effort, he climbed out of bed — it was the first time he'd got up in four days — and he shuffled painfully across the room to get the Mickey Mouse ears he'd bought with Chloe's name embroidered on them and a key ring he bought for me in Hollywood. It was all too much, I'm afraid. Here was this poor little boy on his deathbed and all he could think to do was give me presents. As tough as it was, I pulled myself together, and Damo and I started talking. I learned he had not one girlfriend but *two* — and they were twins. I had to ask him to repeat that to make sure I'd heard him clearly. Of course it was true! If anyone was going to have twins as his girlfriends it was this incredible kid. He had a big basket of chocolates next to his bed and handed me three. When I told Damo I was in serious training for the Griffin fight and couldn't eat chocolates he simply told me one was for Nina, one for Chloe and the other was for the 'boss', Salas. He always thought ahead, Damo. After a few hours the time came to say goodbye but it was hard because I knew this would be the last farewell. I clung to hope, and grasped at straws because I told Damo I wanted him ringside at my next fight. I told him his name was going to be on the trunks I wore into the fight so I could draw upon his courage and strength during the bout. He smiled at that thought, but what really killed was when he signed a photo for me: *To Danny, love lots, Damo*. Christ, it crushed me. I had tried to stay strong for Damo and his family but that instant it overwhelmed me and I sobbed. The kid had so much spirit — so much spark — it was cruel to think this was the end. What the hell had he done to deserve his illness? How could anyone, any superior being, say his fate was fair? I don't know how his family handled it; their strength and resilience was incredible. I had to go. I cuddled Damo; I kissed him and said I loved him. I tried to walk out of the room but I couldn't leave. I just wanted to bundle him up and take him away with me. I walked back a few times, told him I loved him, kissed him and then tried to leave. It took me all my courage to enter his house to see Damo in the first place; I didn't seem to have enough to say my final goodbye. My last vision of Damian was of one hell of a fighter giving me the thumbs up as I walked out the door. Christ knows I bawled.

Outside of his room I apologised to John and Sharon for crying in front of their boy and his siblings because I knew they were trying to be strong for Damo's sake. They told me not to be silly and we hugged. Before I left I asked John to do me one favour and to tell his boy 'he's the toughest motherfucker I know'. John asked if I wanted him to say it in those words and my response was yes. Mates, you see, can talk to one another like that. Even though he was only a kid of 12, I knew that sentiment would mean a lot to Damo. I drove back towards Perth bawling like a baby. It was cruel and it hurt to know nothing could save him.

The next day a media conference had been organised to announce the date of my fight and to talk about Griffin. I knew it was going to be tough because I was still emotional, but I appreciated the presser needed to be done. Not long before it I sent Damo a text that said: 'It was great to see you. Love you little guy.' The reply, however, chilled me to the core. It was from John asking that I call him asap. Damo had died at 1.10am and I was informed I'd been the last person he ever got out of bed for. I spoke to Sharon to let her know my heart was with her and the family. There were lots of tears and while I knew Damian was at least free of that dreadful pain no-one — especially a child — should have to endure, I felt miserable. When I dedicated the fight to Damo during the press conference I choked up and started crying. I couldn't help it because as I sat there talking I thought of how brave he'd been. I'd lost a young mate, his family had lost a special treasure and it felt so wrong. There's a lot to say about people when they're gone and in his short time Damian lit candles in so many people's hearts. In Damian's honour I'm going to repeat what I asked his father to say for me after I saw him that last time: Damo Scott, you are the toughest motherfucker I know. Rest In Peace little buddy. Love you heaps, too.

CHAPTER 46

THE QUICK GREEN FOX

Otis Griffin did a number on the local media a few days before our fight, and had it not been for my experience I could quite easily have fallen for it too. Like most Americans 'Triple OG' wasn't short on confidence so he had no trouble talking up a bloody good fight at out press conference. He promised to give me 'hell' and by the end of his spiel I awarded him extra points for selling himself without resorting to two-bit trash talk. I could sense the media brigade were in tune with his vibe and that they'd been seduced by his charisma.

Griffin played on being the young, hungry fighter, and painted me as being the older pug who'd supposedly dined off fame — ha, if that was the case I should've been anorexic! Something I have tried hard to explain throughout this book is that boxing is a mental game. It's like chess because of the strategy — only the pawns in the square ring belt the crap out of one another in their quest to knock the king (the world champion) over! Griffin was setting up mental traps all over the place for me and I have to admit he'd laid some good ones by referring to some of my fights because it proved he'd at least done his homework. However, I could see some people listening to him were wondering if he'd formulated a 'killer' fight plan. Griffin was wasting his words and mind games on me; I viewed him as the young fox sniffing in the direction of the old fox — the wise one, who, despite years of risks and chances, has managed to avoid being hit by a car on the highway or shot by a farmer protecting his chicken roost. I'd also been in his shoes before, so I remembered what it was like to be an up 'n' comer who craved credibility.

Before the press conference I'd thought about Griffin's attributes. He was an awkward customer who drew his opponents into him and then attacked them with a wicked uppercut and a lovely, crisp jab. He reacted aggressively to being touched up by his opponent, and he also landed in my hometown bearing an impressive enough résumé that showed that from 21 bouts he'd recorded 18 victories — seven by way of KO — one loss and two draws. I picked the 29-year-old Californian prison guard because he was considered a tough contender. He was the reigning NABO light-heavyweight champion, he was rated in the world top 15 by most of the major organisations, and I had it on good authority there was a top-three-ranked contender who refused to fight Griffin because he was considered too dangerous. Any advantage he may have had were his youth, his hunger, his strength and his awkwardness. But I refused to fall into the old trap of paying him too much respect.

My preparation in Sydney really was as close to perfection as I could ever hope for. One night at training, I was so focused I forgot two close mates from Perth, Brooksy and Demon Hayes, were in the gym. I'd just blocked out the fact they were there, but I managed to flick the switch off the instant after I'd finished my warmdown. That's what it was like as I prepared for Griffin: the uptightness I normally felt before a bout was not present. I found outside of training or talking to Salas, I didn't think much about the fight. It was great because a fighter burns up a lot of nervous energy when his mind runs through the upcoming battle over and over again. I was at another level, and I loved it. Salas, however, was concerned that I was going to peak before the bout so we slowed things down. We cancelled an afternoon session one day and I took the following day off. Instead of being flogged in the gym, we took it easy and walked around Bondi Beach and took time out for a coffee and a chat.

I saw Griffin at the weigh-in and after we shook hands and swapped courtesies, I went into lockdown mode. We both easily made weight, but Griffin, who was soaking up the media attention, decided to steal an Ali line and yell 'The champ is here!' He was only being confident, but I told myself he was wrong. The champ was standing on the other side of the room, licking his lips in anticipation at showing the upstart Yank who the boss really was.

I slept restfully that night. My heart rate was spot-on, and I didn't even think about the fight in the hours before we entered the ring. I was so relaxed, even when Salas was wrapping my hands I was laughing and joking and having the time of my life. Ten minutes before I was due to take on the bloke who was promising to beat my brains in because he was younger and hungrier, I could hear the boys chewing on their gum louder than normal, which is a sign of nerves and I know only one remedy for that — to force everyone in the room to dance. So I had all the boys — BG, Dad, Wizza, Noel, Pat, Brooksy, Salas, Angelo, Salty and Billy Bob — groove to 'Blue Monday' by New Order and it was a hoot. I did it before my WBC title shot against Lucas in Canada, but on this particular occasion everyone had to dance solo! My father doubled up to do this crazy dance twice and it made me smile because I'd heard a lot of stories about him being pretty loose as a young bloke and his dancing that night gave me a glimpse into that side of his character. I caught BG's eyes and I could tell he was thinking exactly the same thing as me. We just smiled knowingly and kept dancing. The call 'it's showtime' ended a great little party, and when 'Down Under' blasted through the speakers I marched out to a massive roar of support from the crowd and I fair dinkum loved them for it.

There was a sombre moment, though, and that was when the time came to remember Damo, who'd lost his battle with cancer the previous month. As I'd promised, I had my little mate's name embroidered on my trunks and I knew he was there cheering me on in spirit. I figured he was sitting alongside my Pop, because I know old Tom would have looked after Damo 'up there' for me. Before the fight started we sounded the final 10 count — the ringing of the timekeeper's bell — in honour of Damo. It's normally reserved for departed boxers, but I knew no-one who fought harder — or more bravely — than that 12-year-old. He deserved his salute.

As the last bell sounded I cleared my head by thinking to myself, 'That was for you little guy' and I switched back on to the business of winning my world-title eliminator. As soon as Griffin came forward I speared my jab into his heart and into his left shoulder. The purpose of this was to put him off balance. Griffin expected me to press forward the whole fight, so he was uneasy about coming forward on me because his whole preparation was to out box me off the back foot. I could see I was really frustrating and confusing him. I was also wearing 10-ounce gloves and the power I unleashed in my punches was creating all sorts of damage — mental and physical. Towards the end of the round I speared my jab into Griffin's heart again and it stung him, because he dropped his hands to cover his stomach.

Griffin copped much the same in the second round, but he complained to the referee that I'd rabbit punched, which I can assure you was absolute crap. 'Don't get the referee to change things for you mate,' thought the wise old fox as the young fox yelped and carried on. 'If you're not getting your own way, change it.' As I landed a series of heavy punches on him I could see his will was rapidly draining from his eyes. I was belting it out of him. I was looking at him, waiting to see how much he wanted to win, but I thought his desire was all but extinguished by the end of the second.

To his credit Griffin rallied at the beginning of the third and we opened with a willing toe-to-toe exchange, but I floored him with a *cracker* of a left hook. He climbed back to his feet but after another rally, with Griffin trying to cling to me for survival, I threw the American off like a rag doll and landed a heavy right hand just above the crown of his head. He slid to the canvas. Griffin showed great heart to climb back to his feet but he'd barely had time to blink after the eight count before I was into him again. I was in a frenzy and I could sense the end was near. The doctor was up on the ring, trying in vain to intervene, but I wasn't stopping unless the bell went; the ref dragged me off of my opponent or he went down. As harsh as it may sound they're not only the rules but boxing can be a brutal sport. I continued my assault and collected Griffin with a nice left hook, then a couple of short clubbing rights over his left ear to deposit him on the floor for a third and final time.

The victory sent me into a wild spin. I was ecstatic. It was a crucial win for me and in my excitement I did something I've never done before. I jumped up on the ropes in triumph. I was like a jackrabbit, and in my attempt to involve the crowd I asked if they'd support a world title fight between me and America's IBO champion, Antonio Tarver, at Subiaco Oval. Their response was a resounding yes. After bearhugging my brother and my corner, I made sure Griffin was okay and paid him the respect he deserved. Damo was also in my post-match thoughts, too. 'I want to dedicate this fight to my good little buddy Damo Scott,' I yelled into the ring microphone. 'I love you buddy, I know you sent me that strength.' I also took the opportunity to announce Nina was five months pregnant with our second child.

Afterwards I made the mistake of celebrating with my mates into the early hours of the morning with a bottle of rum. The end result wasn't pretty — a two-day hangover that left me reeling — but even though I felt like a grizzly bear that'd eaten some crook salmon I couldn't stop smiling. I'd already kicked off my campaign to bring Antonio Tarver to Perth by putting calls into his minders. However, it proved a fruitless — and frustrating — time because Tarver's people never seemed committed to the bout. While I was determined to fight Tarver because he was a big name, destiny smiled upon me. The people who managed Croatia's WBC champion Stipe Drews were keen for him to fight me. And they also liked the idea of him punching on in Perth. It was a dream come true.

CHAPTER 47

ONE DOOR CLOSES ...

As of Sunday the 23rd of March, 2008, I have effectively retired from professional boxing. I woke up at 1am Sunday morning with my stomach churning, telling me to hang up my gloves. As you could imagine, I have struggled with the decision as I believe I am at the peak of my career. I have never gone against my gut instincts, and I am not about to start doing that now.

This is a very strong and brave decision to make. Physically I am in the best shape of my life, and mentally I am still as hungry as ever, and my performances in training would suggest I am hitting the peak of my boxing ability, which makes this decision so much harder.

I have been boxing for 16 years, and have given my heart and soul to this great sport. I have given my all, and boxing has given me so much back.

Ever since I was a young kid, I dreamed of being world champion. I have achieved that dream twice, in two weight divisions.

I have had an amazing and memorable career that will stay with me forever. To my supporters — thank you from the bottom of my heart. My fights were for you as well, and I have the best supporters in the world. Through thick and thin you made my journey so exciting.

I am upholding my end of a handshake deal that I had with my father Malcolm before I turned pro. I am getting out on my terms, when I say, with my dignity and respect intact. No-one is going to tap me on the shoulder.

I have made the decision of an intelligent man, a man that has a lot to offer after boxing. I am looking 25 years down the track to when I have grandkids. I want to protect my family forever. I have matured so much, and am now finally living for tomorrow, not today.

I have come a long way since packing up an old Magna, heading across the Nullarbor and living in a one-bedroom flat on the railway line at Ashfield. I will never forget my roots. To everyone who has helped me in my great career, I cannot thank you enough. You all know who you are, and you all know I will never forget you. Thank you to Green Machine promotions, all of my sponsors, and to you, the media, who have backed me all the way.

I am doing what not many professional athletes have done — I am moving into another chapter of my life whilst I am at the top of my game. I am retiring as champion of the world.

This is a happy day for me and my family. To them, thank you from the bottom of my heart. Your support has been overwhelming.

ONE DOOR CLOSES ...

I look forward to continuing contributing to the community in a positive way. I am very proud of the way I have conducted myself both in and out of the ring. I have never taken a back step.

It's my family and friends I live for. I wear my heart on my sleeve.

Someone hand me a vegemite sandwich, 'cause I come from the land Down Under [In reference to my theme song, Down Under *by Men of Work] ...*

— My farewell to arms speech, 25 March 2008.

I woke at 1am on Easter Sunday, my stomach was churning. My gut was screaming at me to listen to it, but I did my best to ignore its message. I climbed out of the bed in my Sydney headquarters and went into the lounge room where I played the DVD of the man I'd fight in my first world title defence, Hugo Garay of Argentina. I liked what I saw. He appeared tailor-made to make me look perfect because of his walk-up style and lack of movement. He came forward and as I watched him in action I could visualise him succumbing to my powerful punches. My gut was still screaming at me when the DVD ended so I watched vision of my previous days sparring session against Laurence Tuausa, and I was stoked to see I'd developed an arsenal of punches that would take me to the next level as a fighter. When Salas, Angelo and I left the gym we were on a real high because with five long hard weeks of preparation still ahead of me that sparring session suggested I was on track to putting in the performance of my life. In the previous 18 months my boxing ability had improved to the point where I was so relaxed in the ring I was able to create even more power and precision. I felt so comfortable in there that even intense sparring sessions were as enjoyable as surfing a perfect 6-foot swell. And Green Machine Promotions had been kept busy because after Garay we'd targeted a series of big fights. The great American Roy Jones Jnr was on our radar, and our initial negotiations suggested he would fight in Perth. My German nemesis Markus Beyer had returned from a brief comeback and had moved up a division to light-heavyweight and, then, of course, there was my rematch with Mundine. It shaped up as the most exciting period of my career but my gut was yelling at me so loudly I could no longer ignore it.

It was time to hang up my gloves.

It was hard to accept my career was over. My heart, body and soul pleaded for me to continue, saying I was at the top of my game and that I have never been better. Yet, my stomach wouldn't stop churning. It was telling me it was time to retire and unlike so many other athletes, I actually listened to its warning. After 16 years as a walk-up fighter, pressing the action, my gut instinct kicked in strongly, telling me it was time to stop living for today and to think about life in 20 to 30 years' time. What was the point in being a former world champion if I didn't know it was my daughter or son I was talking to? What was the point of having a mountain of money if I couldn't remember how I earned it? Boxing is a sport littered with broken men who were once proud lions. Floyd Patterson couldn't recall the name the of fighter he beat to become the then youngest heavyweight champion; the great Muhammad Ali — a man I really admire — finished with Parkinson's disease; Sugar Ray Robinson suffered as a result of the hammerings he copped and I personally know others who have paid a high price for their bravery. A stroll down memory-less lane in my older age holds no appeal for me. I sent Nina a text message at 4am in the hope she may have been awake and feeding Archie. There was no response, so I turned my mobile phone off thinking that it might be better to try and sleep for a few hours and see what my gut feeling was when I woke up. Needless to say it maintained the rage and Nina was stunned to finally hear the news.

Nina asked the most logical question — and that was to see if I wanted to reconsider my decision to have one last bout. Having been with me through my whole journey, Nina knew I would sometimes make rash decisions. She had sided with my head and body, and her reaction annoyed me because while I knew my wife's logic was spot on, I wasn't seeking opinion. I *knew* I had four big fights in me but my gut had made the decision and over the years I've been wise to follow my instinct on such matters.

I rang BG and he was so happy for me. Ecstatic. He thought it was brilliant that I was retiring on my own terms and as the reigning world champion. I rang my father. We had an agreement that he'd tap me on the shoulder when he thought I'd had enough and after I told him I'd beaten him to that punch his tears were like mine, of joy and pride rather than sadness. Keeping my word with my father and making him proud is a feeling I can't possibly describe, and it is certainly one you can't put a dollar figure on. My mother said my decision had added 10 years to her life because she could hardly bear to think about the punishment I'd absorbed in the ring. Most of the other people I spoke to that morning thought it was an early April Fools' Day joke, but it wasn't. I was deadly serious. On 23 March I was about to become the retired world champion and it was tough. It proved to be a day of mixed emotions, but my career as a professional fighter was over. It was hard. The adrenalin surge and empowerment I felt walking into an arena with thousands of people cheering and fanatically supporting me regardless of the result was intoxicating. It is an addictive feeling. Many perks are available to a world champion fighter, but the power I felt at being top dog in my chosen profession was incredible. To walk away from it was extremely difficult, but I was leaving on top of the mountain. Precious few have the strength of character to follow through such a decision. There'll be no return either.

My trainer, Salas, was shocked. I could see it took a few seconds for the news to register with him. He was ten days into preparing his fighter for a world title defence only to hear he would fight no more. He respected my choice and said he realised it was the decision of a wise man. I thanked Salas for everything he'd done. When we hooked up he promised to guide me to a world title and he lived up to his end of the bargain. I like to think we shared a lot of fun along the way, and we forever share a special and rare bond that only a world title can produce. Likewise with Angelo Hyder. H and I had some ridiculously funny times over the years, and had been in what I call some 'beautifully raw' moments together in the build up to and during my big fights. His reaction to my retirement was classic Hyder: 'Beauty mate, now we can get that footy team together we've been talkin' about!'

I also knew no matter how many fights I had, none would eclipse the night of 16 December 2007 when I dominated Stipe Drews and won the world title in front of my home crowd. Thousands from the crowd stayed back and sang the John Williamson song *True Blue*. It was a great occasion, described by a journalist who was ringside as a time of 'rare joy and warmth'. Then Archie was born six days later. It was so perfect and I'm happy to think my decision to retire will ensure I'll carry that memory forever.

On that fateful Easter Sunday in Sydney I watched my old Olympic team-mate Michael Katsidis fight the wily old Cuban Joel Casamayor for the WBO's interim lightweight title. I still watched it through a fighter's eyes. I urged Katsidis to throw more jabs, and I was apparently swaying in my seat to evade the blows the two warriors threw at one another. I had Katsidis ahead on points in the tenth round but a flush punch by the Cuban proved how fickle the sweet science of boxing is. Katsidis was counted out by the referee and I felt for him. I knew how gutted he'd feel — it's a depression that can crush you. I turned the television off to avoid seeing the advertisement promoting my 27 April title defence; the fight that wasn't to be.

On Tuesday, 25 March 2008, I faced a large contingent of media, my family, friends and supporters in Perth to confirm the rumours that had appeared in newspapers on both sides of the continent — I had retired. It was so tough. I prepared a statement, but it was very hard to read through the tears that blinded me. I explained there was no truth to the suggestion that I had some sort of serious illness, but it was instead due to my gut feeling — 'an epiphany' — and that I was happy to be leaving boxing with my dignity and my health intact. People found it difficult to comprehend that I would simply walk away at the pinnacle of my career.

I also made it clear that I appreciated my decision had cost me millions of dollars but there'd be no return to the ring. I never fought for the money side of the sport, though I am pleased my family and I enjoy a great lifestyle that is the result of a lot of hard work and wise investments.

Retiring meant the much-hyped rematch against Mundine would not take place. A few months before I fought Drews, I was asked by Nina if I was given the choice between beating Mundine or winning the world title what would I take. It was a no brainer — I wanted to be the world champion. Though, I took time out to publicly acknowledge Mundine in my press conference to wish him well and to thank him for his rivalry because it made the sport so much more interesting. Sure enough, it was no surprise that he threw it back in my face. Mundine said I was running from a whipping or a similar American trash-talk term. It didn't surprise me. He was behaving like a nagging ex-wife. Still carrying on after a victory and receiving a hefty payout.

Mundine's manager, Khoder Nasser, called a few hours after my retirement speech to advise me to never say never. He has spoken good sense over the years and given me some very sound advice, but we laughed at his suggestion that he would not give up trying to convince me to change my mind. However, the multi-million dollar offer he then made for me to fight Mundine proved Anthony Mundine needed me more than I did him. His cash cow is now kicking back at Scarborough with an exciting new chapter of his life awaiting to unfold. And that will be done with the official WBA world title belt wrapped around my waist for good. Hasta la vista, Choc.

My priority is my family, and it is because of them I will keep in shape. Instead of dealing with some of the sharks that feed off boxing, I'll be dealing with any prospective boyfriends for Chloe. When those boys come knocking at the door I'll be ready if I need to go the knuckle! I'm sure she's going to dread it.

At the beginning of this book I asked what three minutes is out of any person's life. For me it was a time to make every punch count and to give my all when it would have sometimes been so easy to give up. I like to think during the times when it felt as though I had nothing left to give in — and out — of the ring I could always dig deeper.

That, to me, is the power of closed fists and an open heart. It allows you to die a million deaths for pride and honour, family and friends.

CHAPTER 48

HEAVYWEIGHT SUPPORT

I learnt from a very young age that I had to value a mate,
Someone by your side when the wolves are at the gate.
It's so interesting to witness what makes two different people click, what makes their bond so strong, solid as a brick.
You know it is true friendship when time apart does not neglect,
The very reason you love them and that reason is respect.
Like one of my own family members I'm always at your side, buddy,
God help anyone who attempts to harm you, for that, they will end up broken and bloody.
No matter how bad a day may seem, and my patience is put to the test,
Time with you is like a perfect wave, and I'm left feeling on top of the crest.
You bring a smile to so many faces and your presence lights up the room,
Then you crank it up a notch and the atmosphere goes BOOM!
Benny, you are simply a legend who possesses a quality in mates that is a must,
Something I hold so dear, and that is, someone I can trust.

HEAVYWEIGHT SUPPORT

When I wrote this poem for Benny O'Donnell, I was best man at his wedding and it was to celebrate the friendship forged at school, on the footy paddock and while surfing. The sentiment of the poem extends to a lot of people I knew before boxing and to those I befriended along my journey to the world title. One of the great rewards of my life is the people who are important to me. I think it is obvious throughout these pages that my family is my life, and that I'd be willing to bleed for those I consider mates.

I was extremely lucky early in my professional career that the media threw its weight behind me. Boxers find it hard to get recognition in the press, and that frustrates me because very few athletes put everything on the line quite like a fighter.

Jeff Fenech was accustomed to dealing with the media throughout his career and because his Team Fenech fighters enjoyed success there was never a shortage of cameras rolling at the gym. I have a very good relationship with the media and I like to think the reason they've championed my cause over the years is that, apart from my fighting ability, they know the public can relate to me. I think I'm seen as a normal bloke raising a family. I handle being in front of the camera and microphone without saying too many stupid things. I go into battle for the underdog and I'm a larrikin who comes from a blue-collar background with intelligence and respect for others. I believe these are basic qualities that appeal to the average Aussie. I also think it isn't lost on the fight public that, while I try to destroy my opponent in the ring, I'll share a beer with them when the dust has settled.

The media attention certainly helped me on the sponsorship front and over the years I obtained deals with a number of companies, big and small. The first people to align themselves with me were Henk Plug and his son Arie from the Leichhardt Electrical Wholesalers. They took the plunge to support me when I was an unknown.

Jeff suggested I contact them before he left on one of his trips to the US. I jotted down their number and, while I really needed some sponsorship dollars to survive financially in Sydney, it took a while for me to build up the nerve to ring them because I found it hard to cold call a stranger to ask for money. I eventually dialled the number and when a fellow named Arie answered I put on my best phone voice. He told me to come see him.

When I drove to their warehouse in Leichhardt I didn't expect much because I didn't sense any warmth in the half a dozen or so words Arie offered on the phone. Now I know him, I realise that it was just his phone manner — a constant tone of low and busy. Nevertheless, I'd dressed up, dug out my resumé and prepared to present my case. There was no need to offer them a pitch because Henk and Arie had already decided to support me. I'd say that had something to do with Henk's background as a talented boxer, who was selected to represent The Netherlands at the 1960 Rome Olympics before horrific concussion ended his career. The pair's generosity was humbling. When they heard Nina and I were setting up our home in Ashfield they gave us a second-hand fridge and a washing machine to save us from having to buy whitegoods. They invited Nina and me to their homes on countless occasions and made us feel like their own.

I'll never be able to repay the Plugs. They couldn't know of the pressures they saved me and Nina from. I was blessed to meet these wonderful people. They made it possible for me to train at awkward times during traditional business hours and that lifted a heavy weight from my shoulders. Henk's wife, Ria, and Arie's wife, Joanne, have extended the Plugs' support by helping to babysit Chloe. She gets on like a house on fire with Arie's tribe of kids — Bradley, Benny and Jess.

After training I'd go to the warehouse to help out in whatever way I could. I swept the floor, moved boxes, packed the shelves and sometimes, and it was only when they were desperate, I would do deliveries. In those days, Sydney and I just didn't get on. I struggled with the traffic and I'd always get lost. For some reason, it didn't matter if I was despatched to North Ryde or Parramatta, I'd end up at Rockdale, always bloody Rockdale.

Bill Mead from Guardian Solutions Computers, Brian Craig from the concrete company FixCon, and Gavin and Kevin Bloor from the printing company Presfast all came on-board after the Plugs. Bill and Brian came to a couple of my fights with Arie, and because the fellas liked what they saw they supported me. Bill doubled as security for my fights and he didn't miss a bout, regardless of whether it was in Las Vegas, Germany or Montreal, where Billy-Bob spent more time in the air than on the ground, such was his commitment to look after me — a beautiful man with a heart of pure gold. Henk, Arie and Billy-Bob are my three Aussie amigos whom I love dearly.

Brian Craig is an old-school gentleman who was raised on hard work and devotion to his family. A quiet achiever, Brian has always been in the background but his support has never waivered.

Gavin and Kevin Bloor liked to think outside the square when trying to increase my profile. They also took over the production of my fight posters and programs. Two first class gentlemen, they put their heart and soul into helping build my profile.

Steve Bowden approached me with a sponsorship package after he watched me take Jason DeLisle apart in five brutal rounds on the big screen of his hotel, the Ritz Hurstville. We clicked immediately. 'Bowdo' played front row for the Newtown Jets rugby league team and is remembered for his role in one of the sport's most vicious all-in brawls, against Manly in the 1981 preliminary final. Bowdo belted his opposite number, Mark Broadhurst, a Kiwi international who was also a former heavyweight boxer. Bowdo towelled Broadhurst up and gave more than he copped. Broadhurst's head looked as if he'd been attacked by a swarm of wasps when it was over.

Part of our deal was that I could move into the warehouse he bought from the famous radio host and Wallabies coach, Alan Jones. (Jones has been a wonderful supporter over the years and I appreciate the positive comments he's had to say about me.) A part of the building was used as a boxing gym by the legendary trainer Ern McQuillan in the 1940s and 1950s. At the height of its popularity the gym was home to a number of champions, including Vic Patrick, Ron Richards and Jack Hassen. I met Vic Patrick a few times before he passed away and I like to think he'd be happy to know the double-brick walls were shaking again because I'd set up a ring and boxing bag in the building.

Bowdo and his family — wife Louise, daughter Alana and son Tom — are all quality people. They've worked extremely hard for what they have and I respect the fact that, despite their success, they still have their feet on the ground. I always receive solid advice from Bowdo and he knows I listen. Bowdo, you're a champion.

Paul O'Neill from Boost Mobile sponsored me before I fought Jason DeLisle in 2003 and at our first meeting he struck me as being a sharp but polite and humble bloke. After the Mundine fight he invited Nina, Chloe and me to join him and his beautiful clan (wife Jo and their kids — James, Luke, Sam and Ashley) in Fiji to have a break from the world. Believe me, it was great for my soul. We went surfing and Paul hooked me up with his mates from Globe — brothers Steve and Pete Hill — and they gave me the green light to surf Cloudbreak. While I am amazed my phone bill hasn't forced Boost into liquidation, it pleases me to know I have yet another mate for life in Paul. He is a genuine fight fan who also sponsors my good friend, Vic Darchinyan.

Denis 'Macca' McInerney owns a thriving independent Ford dealership in Morley and is a very generous man who works tirelessly for charity. However, I am afraid Nina tested his patience by crashing the two cars he lent us. The first time she ran up the back of another car I walked into his office with my tail between my legs but Denis insisted it wasn't a problem. When Nina crashed Denis' wife's car, I nearly fell off my chair because I was terrified he might've thought we were crashing his vehicles for fun. His right-hand man, Peter Donkin, is a champion bloke who, like Denis, bends over backwards to help me out. Macca used to lend me his personal drive-around car — a tidy supercharged GT. It was either true friendship or the mad Irish in him.

Frank Lawton from Wearside Construction and I connected because he was an amateur boxer back in England, so he not only knows the game but he loves it. When he talks about boxing his eyes beam. Frank is old school, a down the line kind of guy who has based his life on hard work and integrity. He is a staunch supporter and I love watching replays of my fights and seeing Frank leap from his chair to cheer when I either drop my opponent or land a cracker of a punch.

When Jeff McGlinn of NRW Civil and Mining Contracting formed an association with me after I defeated James Crawford in 2005, I never imagined I'd be taken around the world for eight days in a Lear jet. I watched — and learned — as my mate conducted his business in the Maldives, Dubai, Switzerland, Germany, Spain, England, Canada and America. The man is a machine, and I watched in awe as he had powerful heads of industry eating out of his hands. Jeff, like Bowdo and my other sponsors, is a tremendous success story. He pestered a bloke for a job to sell mining equipment and after realising he was good at it, he started his own business. In 13 years he's built for himself a half a billion dollar empire. He comes from humble beginnings and has qualities I admire. He also bats for the underdog, having been one himself. He gives everyone a fair go and I respect that under his tough exterior there's a warm heart. Like me, he has trouble saying 'no' to people who need a hand. It never ceases to amaze me to see Jeff turn up to those meetings overseas with influential businessmen dressed in a Hawaiian shirt and jeans. He has a great gift of reading the play and a good instinct for business. He has fists like King Kong and goes into a seizure when I fight because he gets so excited.

Jack Cowin, founder and owner of Hungry Jacks Australia was my very first sponsor. He supported me when I was an amateur in 1998 and has remained on board ever since. My Dad and Jack go way back. He's an extremely intelligent man who had to make a decision between business or a career in either professional football in Canada or wrestling. I think he made the right call.

David Aris, who worked for Independent Distillers, was another tireless supporter of mine and boxing in general. He always pushed my barrow in trying to sponsor my fights and when he moved on from ID the Green Machine crew — my brother Brendan, especially — were teary-eyed because it meant no more truckloads of free grog.

In Canada, I have a special buddy in Avi Levy who is my North American legal representative. He negotiated my sponsorship deals with Golden Palace. Manfred Pellenger was another great supporter in those early days. I have just formed an alliance with Pro Choice, a national personal protection company where Rob Bird is at the helm. I look forward to my future dealings with the guys.

One person I must thank is John Hall, publican extraordinaire at the Greenwood Hotel in the leafy Perth suburb of Greenwood. I used to watch all the big fights in his pub when I was a kid, and after I won my first professional fight all of my family, friends and supporters gathered there. The crowd grew to such an extent John would put the 'House Full' sign up on the evening of a fight night. It's been brilliant and I appreciate his efforts. To the 'Newtown ping pong ding dong crew' — Nigel 'Evil Kaneival' Harbach, Craig 'Red Cloud' Catterick, Angelo 'H-man' Hyder, Ismael 'Forearms' Salas, Scott 'Firecracker Macka' Mackovich, Jeremy 'Doubles' Blake. Thanks boys for the fantastic rivalry we shared. That garage got a serious going over, and it warms my heart to have taken the trophy back to Perth. Game on, lads!

While so many people have given me heart over the years I would like to individually single out the following: Enzo and George Piazza, Enrico Luchini, Dr Margaret Hislop, James Ballas, Carol Wilson, Patty West, Peter Fiorre, Mikhail Mikhail, Steve Lockart, Lou Manolikos, Harris Mores, Johnno and Russ from Painaway, Edward Gumayashan, Billy Sparsis, Johnny Lheyton, Les Howard, Alex Long, Anthony King, Sam Ayoub, Alf Rabone, Ann from Classic Embroidery, Matt Simms, Habby Heske, Debbie Lothnario, Carmel 'Caramel' Gordon, Curtis Clarke, Scott Boyes, Brendan Daley, Frank Quill, Ray Wheatley, George and Nick Constantine, Matthew Brooks, Pavo from P.Dot Surfboards, Grantlee Kieza, Adrian Warren, Paul Upham, Jonathon Cook, Jay Clarke, Peter Kogoy, David Riccio, Brad Walter, Fiona Rae, Andrew Moore, Johnny Gibbs, Ray Hadley, David Marsh, Wally Foreman, George Grljusich, Dan Ginnane, Joe Cursio, Shane Saltmarsh, Ashleigh Pember,

Vanessa Wilson, Les Howard and Alex Long from Alto's Ford, Paul and Greg Hyde of Just Spectacles Subiaco, Craig Gaspar and Murray McIntyre from Sports Fever, Adrian Mackey — the Primo Concierge, James Crawley and my mates at Quicksilver and Creatures of Leisure, Melissa Young, Jimmy Tansey and Brendan Hartfield from Adidas, Hayden and Curly Piggott, and Greg Piggott who was a big help on my trips to America. Thanks also to the late Steve Spanbrook a great bloke who alongside Dave Brady and John Hall underwrote our first big Perth promotion. While it was a great success the boys took a punt on me. Shane Carvey from Main Event and Fox Sports, David Spencer, Craig Dobbs, Peter Campbell from Main Event and Fox Sports who televised my fights nationally. Thanks to Carl Zappia, Wayne 'Kowabunga' Hughes, David Fleming and my mates at Qantas who treat me so well on all my fights.

To my good friend Nigel Harbach, thanks legend for the years of laughs, gags and good times we shared in the harbour city, and for your genuine support.

To my brother-in-law, Glen, the world's fastest trolleyboy and a man who constantly entertains and amazes me with his humour and daring, thanks Spinner for keeping me in stitches. You're the best, one of a kind.

Many thanks to Sam Ruttyn for providing so many great photographs that were used in this book.

Finally a heartfelt thank you to ABC books, especially Stuart Neal who had faith in *Closed Fists, Open Heart* from day one. To Jody Lee and Brigitta Doyle, thanks so much for your many litres of blood, sweat and tears.

CHAPTER 49

THE GREEN MACHINE

Green Machine promotions, what can I say? Justin 'Molly' Manolikas, Mick Pember, Pauline Wilson and Wayne Loxley — the awesome foursome — did such a fantastic job of promoting my fights for many years. They can add to their already impressive resumes' that they were part of Australian boxing history, not for promoting a world champion but because they also co-promoted the biggest boxing event ever staged in Australia.

I'm certain anyone who attended one of my fights in Perth would attest to my view that the Green Machine crew put on a spectacular show with a great atmosphere. I know whenever I entered the ring is was a truly chest rattling and highly emotive experience for me; it really was the stuff goose bumps were made of.

We came a long way from our first show in 2002, and the guys quickly learned the ropes. Molly did whatever was necessary to keep the show on the road. He has been by my side since we were nine, and I'm certain he'll remain there until we're 99. 'Son' — as I like to call him — have been through thick and thin. He taught me how to fish and has selflessly put me in 'the spot' on countless occasions. If his son Jack is a chip off the old block, I expect my future Tuesday nights will be occupied defending him at tribunal appearances! I expect the old team of Mal and Lou (our dads) will be reignited the day when Molly and I coach Jack and Archie's footy team.

Micky Pember is a classic. I think he was more upset about my retirement than me! He absolutely loved my fights and radiated a rare enthusiasm. Micky was that wrapped after my world title victory I thought he was going to internally combust. We go back a long way, 'Whooska' and I, and I'm proud to call him my mate, and, even better, to have taken his crown as the biggest eater!

'Willo' is the all important female component of the team, and she sometimes displays a pretty hefty 'set' of her own on the occasions when it has been needed. Always on the go, she is an ideas woman who is a valuable asset to the Green Machine team. She possesses a ton of spark and the way her mind ticks over, I'm sure she could nut out the Rubik cube with her eyes closed.

Wayne Loxley has been terrific in organising press conferences and handling media requests. Apart from handing out valuable advice he also calls it how he sees it, I get great amusement from 'Locko' when we share a couple of beers together, because before I know it, he's into me about something that has rubbed him the wrong way and he gives me both barrels whilst pissing himself laughing. Classic.

Rob Brady has been part of the team for a long time and has had a terrific input in assisting Gino on fight day with the merchandise and general tying up of loose ends with DVD's, fight programs and fight posters.

These guys went above the call of duty to ensure my fights were memorable events and that my future was secure. It is very difficult to condense into a few sentences the emotions we shared on fight day. They're emotions that bind us together. I was blessed to have been surrounded by these brilliant and beautiful people, and I will forever embrace the memories I have of them. I look forward, too, to the future that lies ahead with them.

I have the greatest supporters of any boxer. To them I would like to offer a heartfelt vote of thanks because you are the people who made my getting out of bed on a freezing morning worthwhile. You are the people who made getting whacked repeatedly in the face *almost* bearable and you made my job even more satisfying. Without your cheers, without your support, boxing would be a lonesome and tough gig. They say boxing is one man in the ring fighting another, but with you all behind me I have never felt alone. You'll never know the lift you gave me when I walked into the stadium ready to put everything on the line …

From the tradesman with the Green Machine sticker slapped on the back window of his ute to the fanatic who had my signature tattooed on his body and the people who offer a cheery 'onya Danny' when I'm in the street, thank you. You're the people who made the sacrifices mean so much.

The loyalty and respect my supporters have shown me through the ups and downs is humbling — it means the world to me. When I won the world title I said I wanted to hug everyone at Challenge Stadium and I meant it.

The pledge I made long ago was win or lose; I would never let my family, friends and supporters down. I hope they agree I lived up to that.

FIGHT RECORD

Daniel Thomas Green
Born: 09-03-1973
Birth place: Perth, Western Australia
Alias: The Green Machine
Stance: Orthodox
Record: 28 fights. 25 wins (22 KO) + 3 losses

Date	Opponent	City	Result Rds
16-12-07	Stipe Drews (CROATIA)	Perth	W UD 12/12
	WBA light heavyweight world title		
18-07-07	Otis Griffin (USA)	Perth	KO 3/12
	PABA light heavyweight title		
	IBF Pan Pacific light heavyweight title		
	IBO Asia Pacific light heavyweight title		
21-01-07	Paul Murdoch (AUS)	Melbourne	TKO 2/12
	IBF Pan Pacific light heavyweight title		
	PABA light heavyweight title		
20-09-06	Jason DeLisle (AUS)	Perth	KO 9/12
	PABA light heavyweight title		
	IBF Pan Pacific light heavyweight title		
17-05-06	Anthony Mundine (AUS)	Sydney	L UD 12/12
	WBC super middleweight world title eliminator		

CLOSED FISTS, OPEN HEART

Date	Opponent	Venue	Result
11-12-05	Kirino Garcia (MEXICO)	Perth	W UD 10/10
03-07-05	James Crawford (USA)	Perth	KO 5/10
12-03-05	Markus Beyer (GER) WBC super middleweight world title	Zwickau	L MD 12/12
29-09-04	Omar Eduardo Gonzales (ARG)	Sydney	W TKO 5/10
21-03-04	Sean Sullivan (NZ)	Perth	W UD 10/10
20-12-03	Eric Lucas (CAN) WBC-interim super middleweight world title	Montreal	W TKO 6/12
16-08-03	Markus Beyer (GER) WBC super middleweight title	Nuremburg	DQ 5/12
02-06-03	Jason DeLisle (AUS) OPBF super middleweight title IBF Pan Pacific super middleweight title	Sydney	W KO 5/12
15-03-03	Jorge Andres Sclarandi (ARG) IBF Pan Pacific super middleweight title	Perth	W TKO 6/12
19-01-03	Brad Mayo (AUS)	Melbourne	WTKO 1/8
09-11-02	Nico Toriri (INDO) IBF Pan Pacific super middleweight title	Perth	W KO 3/12
27-09-02	Paula Tuilau (FIJI) OBA light heavyweight title	Gosford	W KO 2/12
02-08-02	Joel Burke (AUS)	Sydney	W TKO 4/10
18-05-02	Rhon Roberts (GUYANA)	Las Vegas	W TKO 3/6
19-04-02	Paul Smallman (AUS) IBF Pan Pacific super middleweight title	Sydney	W KO 8/12
08-02-02	Iobe Ledua (FIJI)	Sydney	W KO 2/8
07-12-01	Daniel Tai (NZ)	Wyong	W TKO 6/10
16-11-01	Eni Latu (NZ)	Sydney	W TKO 3/6
26-10-01	Heath Stenton (AUS)	Sydney	W TKO 2/10
18-10-01	Jason Rarere (NZ)	Sydney	W KO 2/6

FIGHT RECORD

28-09-01	Manueli Delaitabua (FIJI)	Sydney	W KO 2/6
03-08-01	Frank Ciampa (AUS)	Sydney	W TKO 2/6
29-06-01	Waqa Kolivuso (FIJI) Green's professional debut	Sydney	W TKO 2/4

Professional titles won by Danny Green:

World Boxing Association (WBA) world light heavyweight
World Boxing Council (WBC) interim world super middleweight
Pan Asian Boxing Association (PABA) light heavyweight
International Boxing Federation (IBF) Pan Pacific light heavyweight
International Boxing Organisation (IBO) Asia Pacific light heavyweight
Oceanic Boxing Association (OBA) super middleweight
Oriental Pacific Boxing Federation (OPBF) super middleweight
International Boxing Federation (IBF) Pan Pacific super middleweight

Amateur Career Highlights

2000 Olympic Games representative	(Sydney)
Gold medal 2000 Oceania Games	(Canberra)
1998 Commonwealth Games representative	(Malaysia)
Gold medal 1997 Arafura Games	(Northern Territory)
Bronze medal 1998 Multi Nations Cup	(United Kingdom)
Bronze medal 1998 Mayors Cup	(The Philippines)
Bronze medal 1998 Liverpool Cup	(United Kingdom)

Australian middleweight title — Arthur Tunstall Cup for 1997 Nationals best boxer

www.ingramcontent.com/pod-product-compliance
Lightning Source LLC
Chambersburg PA
CBHW022038290426
44109CB00014B/894